WORDS FROM
THE MASTER'S COLLECTION

Words From The Master's Collection

(Part 1)

Praise, Testimonies, and Divine Revelations

Vickie Campbell

WORDS FROM THE MASTER'S COLLECTION
Part 1

iUniverse books may be ordered through booksellers or by contacting:

iUniverse
1663 Liberty Drive
Bloomington, IN 47403
www.iuniverse.com
1-800-Authors (1-800-288-4677)

ISBN: 978-1-4917-1704-2 (sc)
ISBN: 978-1-4917-1705-9 (e)

Print information available on the last page.

iUniverse rev. date: 10/26/2016

Scriptures are coming from, The Holy Bible, King James Version. This book has been inspired by the mighty power of the Holy Ghost. Some names have been changed, however, the stories are true.

Contents

THE HEAD

THE COMPASSION, WHICH GOD HAS FOR MANKIND AND THE ACTIONS HE PERFORMED TO PROVE HIS VAST LOVE IS THE GREATEST LOVE STORY THAT HAS EVER BEEN TOLD. HIS BOUNDLESS FEELINGS OF AFFECTION MOTIVATED JESUS (GOD REVEALED IN THE FLESH) TO GIVE HIMSELF AS A LIVING SACRIFICE (ON A CROSS) TO PAY THE PENALTY FOR EACH PERSON'S SINS.

With Sincere Thanks

All praise and glory belong to Jesus Christ. Through His great influence this book was completed. He empowered me to victoriously accomplish each action that needed to be done. Jesus is a powerful God, the Ruler of the universes.

Sincere gratitude is to my loving husband, Stanley Campbell Sr. Stan has always been a good provider; he never pressured me to work. As a result of his faithfulness I had time to do the things that God wanted me to successfully achieve. Recognition is to our children Jason, Whitney, and Stanley Jr. They assisted me over the many years that it took for this vision to be fulfilled.

Acknowledgement belongs to Bishop William L. Bonner; he was the pastor at Solomon's Temple. The Lord blessed me numerous times through Bishop Bonner's preaching, teaching, anointing, and godly wisdom.

Appreciation is to Pastor Lovell Cannon, he is the pastor at True Worship Church. Jesus has spoken many words of encouragement and instructions to me through his preaching and teaching. Pastor Lovell Cannon and First Lady Tina Cannon wrote a chapter that is in this book.

Recognition belongs to Minister Moses Reed; the Lord permitted him to see great potential within me, which was waiting to come out. The first thoughts that came into my mind in regards to writing a book were because of his very inspiring words.

I would like to acknowledge my dear friend, Gwen Cooper. She gave me many words of encouragement over the various years it took for this assignment to be accomplished.

Acknowledgement and expressions of gratitude are to the people (those individuals know who they are) which aided me to complete **WORDS FROM THE MASTER'S COLLECTION (PART 1).** Their faithful actions, wisdom, and words of support were an extreme factor.

Mr. David Campbell (October 2, 1924-April 5, 2014)**, and
Mrs. Vera Campbell** (October 2 1926-March 20, 2015)**,
are missed and forever loved.**

Dedication

This book is dedicated in the memory of my loving mother, Lillian Burt Montgomery. I am also dedicating it to my husband, Stanley Campbell Sr. and our children Jason, Whitney, and Stanley Jr.

This book contains praise, testimonies, and revelation knowledge to the glory of God. Most of the writings discuss different situations, which happened in my life. The remaining divisions are written through His great insight. He longs to reveal mysteries to each person's understanding. *"Even the mystery which hath been hid from ages and from generations, but now is made manifest to his saints. To whom God would make known what is the riches of the glory of this mystery among the Gentiles; which is Christ in you, the hope of glory" (Colossians 1:26-27).*

The directions to eternal life can be found in this book. I asked Jesus to demonstrate His mighty power through the breathtaking actions He gave me to do. God's love, mercy, and amazing grace are within each section. This book has biblical truths that profoundly provide evidence, which proves Jesus Christ is the only sure foundation to eternal life. As an outcome to His powerful and errorless Word, mingling inside of each chapter, it will be very effective in the spiritual and natural realm.

Jesus wanted to reveal Himself to people through my writings. My lack of education did not matter. The Word clearly states, *"Eye hath not seen, nor ear heard, neither have entered into the heart of man, the things which God hath prepared for them that love him. But God*

hath revealed them unto us by his Spirit: for the Spirit searcheth all things, yea, the deep things of God" (1 Corinthians 2:9-10). God was going to endow me with the proficiencies that were required; however, I needed to have confidence in Him. ***"For therein is the righteousness of God revealed from faith to faith: as it is written, "The just shall live by faith" (Romans 1:17).***

People who feel discouraged and sincerely do not know what to do should read this book. Individuals that believe they are alone in a confused and apprehensive world will find hope in these true stories. God wants every person to have high expectations in Jesus' faithfulness. His plan of deliverance and so many other things are revealed in this manuscript.

If someone asked me to describe this book I would compare it to a great treasure chest, which was filled with extremely expensive jewels of all kinds and sizes with the most valuable and extraordinary gem being the direction to eternal life. Jesus will forever receive all praise and glory for executing the breathtaking actions He has triumphantly accomplished through me. **WORDS FROM THE MASTER'S COLLECTION (Part 1)** will do extensive damage to the powers of darkness!

Through God's precise directions, I received understanding on how He wanted me to write this book. Jesus led me to begin and end each section with a scripture. In between the two bible verses He directed me to write true stories or divine enlightenment. Every book that the Lord wants me to write will be completed and extremely effective unto His never ending glory. Appreciation and unlimited praise belongs to Him, He is a powerful God, the King of all kings and His kingdom will never end!

*Blessed be the God and Father of our
Lord Jesus Christ, who hath blessed us with
all spiritual blessings in heavenly places in
Christ: According as he hath chosen us
in him before the foundation of the world,
that we would be holy and without blame before
him in love. Having predestinated us unto the
adoption of children by Jesus Christ to himself,
according to the good pleasure of his will, To
the praise of the glory of his grace, wherein
he hath made us accepted in the beloved.*

Ephesians 1:3-6

Chapter 1

God predestinated the plan of Salvation

And the LORD God said unto the serpent,
Because thou hast done this, thou art cursed
above all cattle, and above every beast of the field;
upon thy belly shalt thou eat all the days of they life.
And I will put enmity between thee and the woman,
and between thy seed and her seed; it shall bruise
thy head, and thou shalt bruise his head.

Genesis 3:14-15

Majesty, dominion, and power belong to the Redeemer of mankind. He paid the price for every person's sins (past, present, and future). Each individual that truly believe and surrenders to Him will receive eternal life.

In the beginning God had a desire (not a need because He is all sufficient) to have fellowship with someone who wanted to have a personal relationship with Him. He created man from the dust of the earth. God breathed into Adam's (the first man) nostrils the breath of life and he became a living soul. The Lord crowned him with His extraordinary glory. He made Eve (the first woman) from one of Adam's ribs.

God told Adam not to eat from the tree of the knowledge of good and evil. The Word declares, *"Of every tree of*

1

the garden thou mayest freely eat. But of the tree of the knowledge of good and evil, thou shalt not eat of it: for in the day that thou eatest thereof thou shalt surely die" (Genesis 2:16-17). Adam told Eve God's command, despite the fatal outcome that would happen she allowed herself to be deceived by the serpent (the devil). *Genesis 3:4-5* tells us, *"And the serpent said unto the woman, Ye shall not surely die: For God doth know that in the day ye eat thereof, then your eyes shall be opened, and ye shall be as gods, knowing good and evil."*

"And when the woman saw that the tree was good for food, and that it was pleasant to the eyes, and a tree to be desired to make one wise, she took of the fruit thereof, and did eat, and gave also unto her husband with her; and he dtid eat" (Genesis 3:6). When Adam fulfilled his wife's selfish and rebellious desire he sinned against God's righteous command.

The Lord has always been rich in mercy; He is the same yesterday, today, and forever. God gave Adam an opportunity to confess the sin he committed. *"And he said, Who told thee that thou wast naked? Has thou eaten of the tree, whereof I commanded thee, that thou shouldest not eat" (Genesis 3:11)?* At that moment God longed to forgive him, however, he would not acknowledge his disobedient deed. The first man refused to ask God to forgive him, instead he uttered, *"The woman whom thou gavest to be with me, she gave me of the tree, and I did eat" (Genesis 3:12).* Adam made an exceptionally unwise decision to blame God and Eve rather than confessing his rebellious action.

Therefore sin came into the world; Adam and Eve died instantly spiritually! God gave them bodies that should have lived forever; nevertheless, the death process began to take place in their natural bodies because of his unwise deed. *"For the wages of sin is death" (Romans 6:23).* Adam's seeds (every person that would be conceived from a man and woman), also received this great penalty. *"For as in Adam all die" (1 Corinthians 15:22).*

As a fatal outcome to Adam's action, the devil received dominion over the earth. He also had authority over every person's natural and eternal existence. *2 Corinthians 4:4* tells us, *"Satan, who is the god of this world, has blinded the eyes of those who don't believe."* An enormous price had to be compensated in order for mankind to be put back into the right standings with the Lord. They could not obtain restoration until that massive payment was paid in full. A sinless person had to willingly offer themselves to God as a living sacrifice. However, there wasn't a human being on earth who could perform that action because every individual was born in sin!

As an overwhelming effect of God's vast Agape love, He was willing to endure that chastisement. For Him to legally come to earth He had to have a human body because God is an invisible Spirit (*St. John 4:24*). Through the power of the Holy Ghost, He manifested Himself (in the form of His own Son, Jesus) inside the womb of a virgin. It is written, *"Then said Mary unto the angel, How shall this be, seeing I know not a man? And the angel answered and said unto her, The Holy Ghost shall come upon thee, and the power of the Highest shall over shadow thee, therefore also that holy thing which shall be born of thee shall be called the Son of God" (Luke 1:34-35).* Nine months later Jesus was born!

At an appointed time Jesus' ministry began. He preached **"The Kingdom of God"** is at hand. The Anointed One did great and mighty wonders to the glory of God. John's disciples asked Him, *"Art thou he that should come, or do* *we look for another? Jesus answered and said unto them, Go and shew John again those things which ye do hear and see. The blind receive their sight, and the lame walk, the lepers are cleansed, and the deaf hear, the dead are raised up, and the poor have the gospel preached to them" (Matthew 11:3-5). "And there are also many other things which Jesus did, the which, if they should be written every one, I suppose that even the world itself could not contain the books that should be written" (St. John 21:25).*

Jesus entered the natural realm to pay the penalty of sin, His blood had to come out of His body, *"And almost all things are by the law purged with blood; and without shedding of blood is no remission" (Hebrews 10:34).* He suffered death. *"And being found in fashion as a man, he humbled himself, and became obedient unto death, even the death of the cross" (Philippians 2:8).* Jesus' atonement is forever! The Word profoundly states, *"But Christ being come an high priest of good things to come, by a greater and more perfect tabernacle, not made with hands, that is to say, not of this building. Neither by the blood of goats and calves, but by his own blood he entered in once into the holy place, having obtained eternal redemption for us" (Hebrews 9:11-12).*

Before the death of Jesus an animal was sacrificed to make atonement for the sins of the children of Israel, God's chosen people. A high priest would go into the "Most Holy Place" where only he was allowed to enter. He sacrificed two animals (without spots or blemishes), one for the people's sins and the other for his sins. *Hebrews 9:7.* However, that atonement was only temporal; it had to be done once a year. Gentiles were not included in the promises that God confirmed to Israel which made them have no part of the atonements that were made. *Ephesians 2:11-12* tells us, *"Wherefore remember, that ye being in time past Gentiles in the flesh, who are called Uncircumcision by that which is called the Circumcision in the flesh made by hands. That at that time ye were without Christ, being aliens from the commonwealth of Israel, and strangers from the covenants of promise, having no hope, and without God in the world."*

Christ's birth, death, and resurrection are the most significant events that ever took place! Through Jesus' birth God legally came to earth as a man to redeem mankind. *"And without controversy great is the mystery of godliness: God was manifest in the flesh" (1 Timothy 3:16).* As a powerful effect to the Lord giving Himself as a sacrifice, He triumphantly defeated the powers of sin, taking back the authority that Satan had over mankind. *"And, having made peace through the blood of his cross, by him to reconcile all things unto himself; by him, I say, whether they be things in earth, or things in heaven, And you, that were sometimes alienated and enemies in your mind by wicked works, yet now hath he reconciled" (Colossians 1:20-21).* His resurrection proved His sacrifice was accepted, *"For if, when we were enemies, we were reconciled to God by the death of his Son, much more, being reconciled, we shall be saved by his life. And not only so, but we also joy in God through our Lord Jesus Christ, by whom we have now received the atonement" (Romans 5:10-11).*

Jesus victoriously became the Head of a new creation. His obedient and unwavering exploits were the greatest acts of love that has ever been performed! *"In this was manifested the love of God toward us, because that God sent his only begotten Son into the World, that we might live through him. Herein is love, not that we loved God, but that he loved us, and sent his Son to be the propitiation for our sins" (1 John 4:9).*

Each individual that believe (**God will judge every person's actions**), repent, and receives Jesus as their personal Saviour, names will be written in the **"Lamb's Book of Life."** *"Therefore being justified by faith, we have peace with God through our Lord Jesus Christ" (Romans 5:1). Much more then, being now justified by his blood, we shall be saved from wrath through him" (Romans 5:9).* Surrender your life to Jesus today; He is the **Author of Eternal Life.**

Each person whose name is not in **"The Book of Life"** will be judged on **"Judgment Day."** They are going to receive the second death and be perpetually separated from a loving, holy, and righteous God. The Word strongly cries out, *"And I saw the dead, small and great, stand before God; and the books were opened: and another book was opened, which is the book of life: and the dead were judged out of those things which were written in the books, according to their works" (Revelation 20-12). "And death and hell were cast into the lake of fire. This is the second death. And whosoever was not found written in the book of life was cast into the lake of fire" (Revelation 20:14).*

"And he laid hold on the dragon, that old serpent, which is the Devil and Satan, and bound him a thousand years. And cast him into the bottomless pit, and shut him up, and set a seal upon him, that he should deceive the nations no more, till the thousand years should be fulfilled: and after that he must be loosed a little season" (Revelation 20:2-3). With God's final ruling relating to Satan being, *"And the devil that deceived them was cast into the lake of fire and brimstone, where the beast and the false prophet are, and shall be tormented day and night for ever and ever" (Revelation 20:10).*

*Fear not, I am the first and the last. I am he
that liveth, and was dead; and, behold, I am alive for
evermore, A-men'; and have the keys of hell and of death.
And behold, I come quickly and my reward is with
me to give every man according as his work shall be.*

Revelation 1:17-18, 22:12

God predestinated the plan of Salvation.

*A father of the fatherless, and a judge
of the widows, is God in his holy habitation.*

Psalm 68:5

All praise and glory belongs to God. He has a great longing to reveal His unrestricted and endless love to each person. The Lord of Host wants to be a Faithful Heavenly Father to a fatherless generation.

My father died when I was a little girl, his death made it impossible for me to know the love of a father. A great void grew within because of his absence. He was not there to do the obligations and honors that God gave him to perform on my behalf. While growing up I had a deep longing to feel his presence, those profound emotions were ignored for many years. I did not feel totally connected to my brothers and sister. Their father was very kind; nevertheless, a vast empty space existed inside of me, which needed to be overflowed by my biological father's love and concern.

A father should love, provide, and protect his daughter or daughters. He ought to be a righteous, loving, and faithful man. His presence stops serious and destructive issues from taking place. A father is an extremely vital component in a family unit. The image he gives should help them to recognize the right or wrong men that will one day attempt to come into their lives.

It is very important for boys and young men to have a loving, understanding, and hardworking father. He has a great responsibility to be a good example in every manner.

Each boy needs a father to influence them to develop into the greatest men that they can become. His duty is to say encouraging and edifying words to his son or sons. Fathers who are not exemplifying those important qualities are demonstrating the wrong behavioral traits. Always remember, boys usually act like their fathers good or bad! Men who are guilty in this area need to ask the Lord to help them to successfully accomplish this extremely important duty.

God longs to deliver people that are having difficulties because their fathers were not in their lives. He wants to heal every issue. Through Jesus Christ, He made a way for each person to be a part of His family. The Word tells us, *"According as he hath chosen us in him before the foundation of the world, that we should be holy and without blame before him in love: Having predestinated us unto the adoption of children by Jesus Christ to himself, according to the good pleasure of his will" (Ephesians 1:4-5).*

God wanted me to receive Him as my Heavenly Father. In the beginning doing that was so difficult; I had many hidden thoughts, which confused my mind. Nevertheless, those mixed up deliberations did not sadden, provoke, or offend Him. Through the Lord's boundless compassion, He showed His love to me in a very personal way. Jesus openly demonstrated His great concern; He has an endless and intense love and kindness.

Prior to the foundation of the world, God made a choice to love every person with an unconditional, unchanging, and undeserved love. The Lord's infinite and boundless compassion motivated Him to come to earth (in the image of His own Son) to give His life as a living sacrifice to pay the penalty of sin, and to brake the power that sin had on the human race. *"Hereby perceive we the love of God, because he laid down his life for us" (1 John 3:16).* God is a loving and compassionate Heavenly Father; He has an extreme desire to take care of each person's needs. His utmost objectives are to extend love, mercy, and restoration. The Lord longs to forgive, deliver, and grant His amazing grace to each individual.

> *Behold, what manner of love the Father hath bestowed upon us, that we should be called the sons of God: therefore the world knoweth us not, because it knew him not.*
>
> *1 John 3:1*

God predestinated the plan of Salvation.

*Be careful for nothing; but in every thing by
prayer and supplication with thanksgiving let
your requests be made known unto God. And the
peace of God, which passeth all understanding, shall
keep your hearts and minds through Christ Jesus.*

Philippians 4:6-7

Genuine words of appreciation belong to JEHOVAH-SHAMMAH (The Lord who is always present)!

There was a time I permitted myself to be curious relating to things, which had bad consequences. At a very young age Stan and I met, deep feelings began to grow inside of me for him. Those confused sentiments should not have been allowed to develop and intensify. The two of us were not mentally or emotionally strong enough for that type of relationship to be taking place. He eventually attempted to kiss me, and our sexual curiosity began.

It was close to a year before Stan and I had sex, the very first time that we were sexually active I got pregnant. Expecting a baby at the youthful age of sixteen was truly unbelievable and extremely depressing. My untimely pregnancy brought overwhelming feelings of embarrassment.

For a couple of months I did not say anything to Stan about me being pregnant, uneasiness and fear besieged my mind relating to how he would react. While we were talking on the telephone one night I somehow became courageous enough to express to him our difficulty. After those words were clearly said to Stan, he told me he had to get off of the phone.

It was at least three months before we had any type of communication. Stan's actions made me feel very humiliated and used. This was a challenging time in my life. The young man whom I truly loved did not appear to have feelings for me, neither did he show any interest, in regard to our unborn baby. I felt hopeless and unwanted; nevertheless, my sad and confused emotions did not seem to be a concern to him.

On April 16 our baby was born, however, Stan did not know about the things, which took place. My mother, stepfather, and brother were at the hospital with me. In the beginning I wanted to have an abortion. It would have haphazardly resolved this complicated diagnosis; my mother stopped me from making that unwise decision.

While being in the hospital a great longing existed in me, which desired to call Stan and tell him, his first child was born. Brokenhearted feelings intensified, unforgiving emotions stopped me from telling Stan things he had a right to know. I had a new born baby; though, it felt like we were abandoned by his father. This was a life changing consequence to our sexual curiosity.

Praise and glory belong to God, He found a way to use each unwanted issue that occurred unto His awesome glory. When those unpleasant circumstances were happening I felt confused, unhappy, and fearful. Uncertainty amplified because the problems were magnified. The Lord had to teach me how to victoriously go through each difficulty.

When a single man and woman kiss each other before marriage their actions will give them a greater longing to have sex. Two unmarried individuals' sexual desires being fulfilled explains the high number of pregnancies that are out of holy matrimony. Not attempting to count the uncountable number of babies, which have been aborted as a result to those lustful longings being satisfied.

In trying times people should not allow themselves to be stunned by fear or doubt. They need to center their attention on God's Word and the victory Jesus received at Calvary. He made a way for every person that truly believes the exploits He accomplished (and sincerely accepts Him as their Saviour) to receive triumph in each situation.

> *Finally, brethren, whatsoever things are true, whatsoever things are honest, whatsoever things are just, whatsoever things are pure, whatsoever things are lovely, whatsoever things are of a good report; if there be any virtue, and if there be any praise, think on these things.*

> *Philippians 4:8*

God predestinated the plan of Salvation.

In whom also we have obtained an inheritance,
being predestinated according to the purpose of him who
worketh all things after the counsel of his own will.

Ephesians 1:11

Glory and praise belong to God. He is Jehovah Rapha, the God that heals.

Stan and I stayed out one night getting high and attempting to gratify our lustful longing. After going home the next morning, to my dismay I fainted. The E.M.S unit rushed me to Outer-Drive Hospital. An emergency doctor declared I experienced a seizure.

They admitted me into the hospital, several x-rays were taken. Dr. Freeland declared something was detected on the left side of my head; he also proclaimed I needed to have head surgery. The surgical procedures were too complicated for him to perform so he referred me to a neurologist. After going to see that doctor, he agreed with the diagnosis, which had previously been given.

Days after being in a different hospital two nurses took me to a room so I could be prepared for surgery. The surgeon previously proclaimed all of my hair had to be shaved off; before he began to execute that task, I asked him if he could shave off only half. The doctor said it was possible because he also had barber's license. His words made me laugh; they additionally broke the apprehension, which started to develop.

Recalling those exceptionally difficult days of suffering, I truly believed Stan began to love me. My weak condition penetrated his heart. When those things were happening he was very concerned, despite the many ups and downs which took place in our relationship.

While the doctor was performing the operation my life could have been taken. All praise and all glory belongs to God because He did not permit a very premature and unprepared death to take place. Jesus has always been so faithful. The Lord did not only want to heal me; He also desired to restore my sin sick soul.

But God hath chosen the foolish things of the world to confound the wise; and God hath chosen the weak things of the world to confound the things that are mighty.

1 Corinthians 1:27

God predestinated the plan of Salvation.

*And you shall know the truth, and
the truth shall make you free.*

St. John 8:32

Praise and honor belong to Jesus. He wants to free each person from the bondage of sin.

My life felt like a roller coaster which was running vigorously out of control, conviction began to overwhelm me pertaining to new, however, not completely understood spiritual revelations. I realized actions such as fornication (sex before marriage), getting high, lying, and so on were against God. The greatest captivity that had me imprisoned when those things were taking place was my relationship with Stan. He and I had passionate feelings for each other, which should not have been taking place; those sexual sensations being fulfilled made us parents at a very young age.

As a result to new spiritual disclosures, I decided to submit to Jesus. Days after that decision was made Stan came to visit. He said the right words, one thing lead to another, and he left me feeling hopeless and overcome in defeat. Sinful yearnings began to take control again; and I no longer had a desire to live in a righteous manner.

The conceiving of two more children was another product of our lustful wishes being satisfied. We had been living this way for too many years, and nothing appeared to be going right. At that time I truly believed my deep feelings of love for him was enough. Though the difficulties and unhappiness increased so intensely, I finally asked God to put us together in marriage or to separate us.

Months later I remembered my request and now questioned the Lord again. Following those thoughts, Jesus spoke to me for the very first time. He said, "Vickie get saved. If Stan loves you he will marry you, however, if he does not he will leave you." My boyfriend had to make a choice. After Stan was given an ultimatum we were married two months later.

A person should never put off yielding their life to Jesus. As soon as they feel themself being drawn by His massive power he or she ought to surrender. Always remember today is the day for salvation because tomorrow is not promised to anyone. Do not be disobedient; Jesus is the only way that a person can receive eternal life!

> *Trust in the LORD with all thine heart; and lean not unto thine own understanding. In all thy ways acknowledge him, and he shall direct thy paths.*
>
> *Proverbs 3:5-6*

God predestinated the plan of Salvation.

No weapon that is formed against thee shall prosper;
and every tongue that shall rise against thee in judgment
thou shalt condemn. This is the heritage of the servants of
the LORD, and their righteousness is of me, saith the LORD.

Isaiah 54:17

Jesus is a Strong Deliverer, eternal praise belong to Him now, and throughout perpetuity.

The Lord wanted to deliver me from issues that were deeply embedded in my mind; I was being controlled by shame. Many bad outcomes came from the mental assaults that took place. Condemnation imprisoned me; those attacks were being controlled by the powers of darkness.

I went to my father's house to stay with him one summer. Days after being there he needed to take care of some business, so I had to go to a cousin's house for a couple of hours. She unwisely left her husband and me alone in a room, and he began to touch my body in the wrong way. The things that took place were very frightening and confusing. Years later Satan assaulted me through a neighbor, I could not believe this nightmare was happening again. The man had a wife and appeared to be nice; he looked like a trustworthy person, nevertheless, my neighbor's actions were being regulated by the devil; he ruled his life.

While walking through our neighbor's living room (trying to go home) he began to touch me. Nothing was said about the things that happened. After it occurred more than one time I began to tell half true stories to a friend.

The stories somehow got back to my mother; she did not believe those violating and extremely hard to understand actions took place. Her trusting a man who appeared to be kind was unwise. My mother's decision gave him another opportunity to touch me in the wrong way.

After sometime passed, I realized wrong and abusive things that happened to a child while they are growing up could have extremely bad effects on their life. Feelings of guilt and fear existed in my mind for too many years. The things which transpired were extremely disturbing. An aftermath that came from those concerns made it very difficult for me to trust men.

God began to deliver me from a great captivity, my unwanted secrets had to be confronted and overcome. I could not allow myself to be restricted by them another day. Whitney (my daughter) was the first person that I told. Stan also needed to know about the things which happened; those concerns were revealed to him through a letter.

I realized that my words were also releasing me from a great bondage. It is written, *"And they overcame him by the blood of the Lamb, and by the word of their testimony" (Revelation 12:11).* While being at church one Sunday, a thought came from within to testify about the freedom I was now feeling. At the same time, a condemning oppression attempted to overwhelm me. Nevertheless, I stood up and testified to the glory of God. The Word tells us, *"There is therefore now no condemnation to them which are in Christ Jesus" (Romans 8:1).*

At this chapter in my life Jesus could use me to talk to children, women, and men that are having issues because they were sexually abused. I would tell them, they were not guilty in regards to the extreme things which took place! Neither should he or she permit those unfair and offensive circumstances to overwhelm or control them in any manner. For freedom to truly be received, from the imprisonment that comes from being sexually abused, they must forgive the abuser or abusers.

I have forgiven the men that molested me. There is not any anger or hatred in my heart towards them. *"For if ye forgive men their trespasses, your heavenly Father will also forgive you. But if ye forgive not men their trespasses, neither will your Father forgive your trespasses" (Matthew 6:14-15).* God would forgive them if they repented with a godly sorrowfulness and truly desire to change.

I would declare God's infinite, unconditional, and unchanging love to the people that were abused. It is written, *"But God commendeth his love toward us, in that, while we were yet sinners, Christ died for us" (Romans 5:8).* In another place it states, *"And God shall wipe away all tears from their eyes; and there shall be no more death, nether sorrow, nor crying, neither shall there be any more pain: for the former things are passed away" (Revelation 21:4).* Jesus' desire is to save every individual.

People should never permit themselves to be measured by bad things that happened in their past, education, wealth, beauty, or so on. Having a personal relationship with Jesus ought to be each person's greatest concern. The Lord wants to deliver every sinner from their wrong way of living. The Messiah longs for them to surrender to Him. His Word tells us, *"And as it is appointed unto men once to die, but after this the judgment. So Christ was once offered to bear the sins of many; and unto them that look for him shall he appear the second time without sin unto salvation" (Hebrews 9:27-28).*

Moreover whom he did predestinate,
them he also called: and whom he
called, them he also justified: and whom
he justified, them he also glorified.
What shall we then say to these things?
If God be for us, who can be against us?

Romans 8:30-31

*B*lessed be the God and Father of our
Lord Jesus Christ, which according to his
abundant mercy hath begotten us again
unto a lively hope by the resurrection of
Jesus Christ from the dead. To an inheritance
incorruptible, and undefiled, and that fadeth
not away, reserved in heaven for you. Who are
kept by the power of God through faith unto
salvation ready to be revealed in the last time.

1 Peter 1:3-5

Chapter 2

Receive deliverance

(from sin and its penalty) and power!

Let your light so shine before men,
that they may see your good works, and
glorify your Father, which is in heaven.

Matthew 5:16

Praise and glory belong to Jesus Christ. He is a penetrating light which shines intensely in a world full of darkness.

The weekend after Stan and I were married, we stayed at an exclusive hotel. It had a living room, bedroom, two bathrooms, and a small kitchen. Two of our friends who were married came to the hotel to celebrate with us. When those things took place I was attempting to stop smoking cigarettes, though one of them had an extra pack. The next evening I made an unwise decision to smoke marijuana. God freed me from both of those bad habits through His mighty power.

Stan decided to go to our house; while he was gone I began to think. To my surprise a strong desire came inside of me that longed to be a virgin, however, that was impossible. We had been having sex for many years, and were the parents of three children. In the beginning of our relationship I did not know how important it was for us not to be sexually active.

The Lord wants each young woman who is a virgin to be faithful and refuse to compromise! Do not surrender yourself to a man before marriage; regardless to how difficult it might become.

A bride's virginity is the most excellent gift in which she can give to her husband on their wedding night. Jesus did not intend for two people to have sex before that marvelous union took place. If you are sexually before marriage get control over those desires. The Lord wants to teach each person how to maintain themselves.

Ladies, the right men will respect your choice not to have sex before marriage. When young women wait for the men, He has for them, the unnecessary difficulties which occur in many marriages will not take place in theirs. Jesus longs to bless each couple that was obedient in this manner with a wonderful, overwhelming, and exhilarating sexual experience on their wedding night.

The man that does not value your decision to wait (until after marriage) to experience sex does not truly love you. He loves himself and his pleasure seeking desires being satisfied. This type of man will gratify those feelings with you or any other woman that allows him to use them. Be extremely cautious, his intentions are to use misleading devices such as lying words, deceiving actions, money, and gifts attempting to weaken you. Two people having sex before marriage is a sin before God do not put your soul into eternal jeopardy!

Not too many days after my husband and I got home Jesus asked me, "How will Stan follow you if your light is not shining?" Those words were said twice, He was referring to the wrong things I did while we were at the hotel. Jesus wanted me to know that Stan would be observing my actions. I had to learn how to be a good example, so he would one day follow me to Jesus.

Believers should live holy and surrendered lives; their virtuous illustrations will direct people to Jesus. He longs to deliver mankind from the authorities of darkness. The Lord and His angles rejoice and receive great joy, when individuals are being saved. Majesty, praise, and recognition without ending belong to Him because of the victorious actions He has accomplished and the important duties He entrusted His beloved to execute. **Let your light shine intensely unto the glory of God.**

> *To open their eyes, and to turn them from darkness to light, and from the power of Satan unto God, that they may receive forgiveness of sins, and inheritance among them which are sanctified by faith that is in me.*
>
> *Act 26:18*

Receive deliverance
(from sin and its penalty) and power!

*Then said Paul, John verily baptized with the baptism
of repentance, saying unto the people, that they should
believe on him which should come after him that is, on
Christ Jesus. When they heard this, they were baptized in
the name of the Lord Jesus"*

(Act 19:4-5).

Every knee shall bow and every tongue shall confess that
Jesus Christ is Lord, to the glory of God. Praise, glory, and
dominion belong to Him now and forever.

One Sunday morning my mother, two brothers, sister-in-
law, and I visited a new church. Bishop Bonner preached
an insightful and extremely life changing message. After
his sermon, he asked if anyone wanted to be baptized in
the name Lord Jesus Christ. A sincere desire existed within
me that longed to submit to God in every way. Many years
before this happened; I was baptized in the name of the
Father, and of the Son, and of the Holy Ghost. When those
things were taking place a thought went through my mind
declaring I needed to be baptized again.

I began to meet people who told me that every person
needed to be baptized in the name of Jesus Christ. **Acts
2:38** strongly confirmed their words. It unquestionably
states, **"Then Peter said unto them, Repent, and be
baptized every one of you in the name of Jesus Christ
for the remission of sins, and ye shall receive the gift
of the Holy Ghost."** As an effect of me not completely

understanding this revelation, confusion began to grow inside of my mind relating to the way in which I needed to be baptized.

I had read **Matthew 28:19** many times. It proclaims, ***"Go ye therefore, and teach all nations, baptizing them in the name of the Father, and of the Son, and of the Holy Ghost."*** My lack of understanding led me to believe the Scriptures were contradicting themselves. Years later God revealed to me He is Jesus manifested in the flesh. Father, Son, and Holy Ghost are not proper names but titles, expressing the great-three fold manifestation of ***GOD (the Father in Creation), SON (in Redemption), and HOLY SPIRIT (in the Regeneration in the church).*** When a person is baptized in the name Lord Jesus Christ **Matthew 28:19** is being fulfilled.

I asked Jimmy and Dwight, if they wanted to get baptized. To my disappointment both of them said no. Their reply helped me to realize this was an extremely important action each individual had to execute on their own. I swiftly stood up, and began to walk to the front of the church; my desire was to be obedient to God.

When I got to the front of the church a missionary led me to a minister. With a strong voice he asked, "Would you like to repent for your sins and be baptized in the name Lord Jesus Christ for the remission of your sins?" My answer was a resounding yes, after I changed clothes; a different minister was patiently waiting in the baptism pool. Following me getting inside of it he said, "I baptize you in the name Lord Jesus Christ for the remission of your sins," he then emerged my body into the water.

While being under the water it felt like something very powerful came inside of me. My body jerked and became as stiff as a board. At that time I did not truly understand the things which were taking place, though, I believed something very significant occurred. All credit belongs to Jesus Christ; He has an uncontainable and miraculous power.

> *"And whatsoever ye do in word or deed,*
> *do all in the name of the Lord Jesus, giving*
> *thanks to God and the Father by him"*

> *(Colossians 3:17).*

Receive deliverance
(from sin and its penalty) and power!

I indeed baptize you with water
unto repentance: but he that
cometh after me is mightier than I,
whose shoes I am not worthy to
bear: he shall baptize you with
the Holy Ghost, and with fire.

Matthew 3:11

Eternal praise belongs to Jesus Christ, He is a consuming fire. Jesus triumphantly received total victory over sin and the powers of darkness at Calvary.

Mrs. Juanita Cooper gave my children and me a ride to church many times. One of Stan's friends introduced us to each other; they both attended Solomon's Temple. Through Sister Cooper, I was taught many spiritual truths.

Pastor Bonner preached another life altering message. After service Sister Cooper asked me if I wanted to receive the Holy Ghost. My answer was yes, we went to one of the rooms where people go to pray and glorify God. She directed me to humble myself before Him. I began to say Hallelujah. Hallelujah is the highest praise a person can give to the Lord, which only He can receive!

In the beginning my thoughts were going in so many directions. Not long after saying Hallelujah these words began to come within me, Jesus I love you and I need you. Not long after thinking on those contemplations, my thoughts began to focus and mediate on the Lord. The Word tells us, *"Commit thy works unto the LORD and thy thoughts shall be established" (Proverbs 16:3).*

Something extraordinary started to take place. To my amazement, Jesus filled me with the Holy Ghost, and I began to speak with other tongues (a heavenly language). The Scriptures proclaim, *"And they were all filled with the Holy Ghost, and began to speak with other tongues, as the Spirit gave them utterance" (Act 2:4).* Being able to speak in an unknown dialect was an astonishing and supernatural action taking place. Words were being said by me that no one understood.

The Holy Ghost is helping me to live in a manner that is glorifying to Jesus Christ. My desire is to act in a demeanor which will always be pleasing to Him. It is written, *"But ye are a chosen generation, a royal priesthood, an holy nation, a peculiar people; that ye should shew forth the praise of him who hath called you out of darkness into his marvelous light" (1 Peter 2:9).*

After true repentance develops inside a sinner, they should ask the Lord to forgive them (for their sinful way of living), and accept Jesus as their Saviour! *St John 14:6* tells us, *"I* (Jesus) *am the way, the truth, and the life; no man cometh unto the Father but by me.* At that moment a transformation takes place in their heart. They should diligently seek to be filled with the Holy Ghost. Jesus is going to complete each action, which needs to be done on their behalf. *"Being confident of this very thing, that he which hath begun a good work in you will perform it until the day of Jesus Christ" (Philippians 1:6).*

Neither is there salvation in any other:
for there is none other name under heaven
given among men, whereby we must be saved.

Act 4:12

Receive deliverance
(from sin and its penalty) and power!

*But ye shall receive power, after that
the Holy Ghost is come upon you: and ye
shall be witnesses unto me both in Jerusalem,
and in all Ju-dae'-a, and in Sa-ma-ri-a,
and unto the uttermost part of the earth.*

Act 1:8

All majesty belongs to God now and throughout time. Appreciation is deeply embedded inside of my heart because He chose me to be a follower of Jesus Christ.

"If any man thirst, let him come unto me, and drink. He that believeth on me, as the scripture hath said, out of his belly shall flow rivers of living water" (St. John 7:37-38). Jesus wants to satisfy the hunger and thirst, which is inside of every person's heart. People have unsuccessfully attempted to gratify that inner identity with all types of sins such as adultery, fornication, homosexuality, pornography, and so on. They have exalted themselves with their worldly possessions, educations, beauty, and money. The spirit of darkness has captivated individuals with unforgiveness, drugs, lust, hatred, and many other ungodly characteristics. God's Spirit living inside a person is the only way that vacant place can be completely satisfied.

People receiving God's Spirit is one of the most significant, life altering, and totally fulfilling occurrence that could ever happen. His powerful supremacy gives them unlimited

WORDS FROM THE MASTER'S COLLECTION

power. Their purposes are to effectively witness the gospel of Jesus Christ, devastate the influences of darkness, and to exercise that authority to the fullest magnitude.

"And when the day of Pentecost was fully come, they were all with one accord in one place" (Acts 2:1). And they were all filled with the Holy Ghost, and began to speak with other tongues, as the Spirit of God gave them utterance" (Acts 2:-4). There are individuals who believe a person can receive the Holy Ghost without them having the confirmation of speaking in an unknown tongue. Though when believers received God's Spirit as it is recorded in *Acts 2:4, Act 10:45-46,* and *Acts 19:6* they all spoke with another tongue as His Spirit gave them the ability. *Acts 2:8-11* tell us some of the languages that they spoke.

I will say it again, people receiving God's Spirit is one of the most significant, life altering, and totally fulfilling occurrence that could ever happen. His powerful supremacy gives them unlimited power. Their purposes are to effectively witness the gospel of Jesus Christ, devastate the influences of darkness, and to exercise that authority to the fullest magnitude!

When an individual is making petitions in unknown tongues the Holy Ghost is having a private and very authoritative conversation with God that only He can comprehend. *"For he that speaketh in an unknown tongue speaketh not unto men, but to God: for no man understandeth him; howbeit in the spirit he speaketh mysteries" (1 Corinthians 14:2).* Jesus can use a person's mouth to make requests for people who are on the other side of the earth. As an effect to the triumph He accomplished at Calvary, the Holy Spirt will be at liberty to give those individuals victory.

The devil wants every person to be totally confused and defiant in regards to them speaking in other tongues. The Holy Ghost is a powerful extraordinary Entity that will help each saved being receive endless victory. Satan feels very perplexed when individuals are praying in unfamiliar tongues, because he cannot understand or stop the verbal statements that are being uttered. Speaking in another tongue is a heavenly language, which is controlled by the awesome supremacy of God.

An individual being filled with the Holy Ghost is God's gift to mankind, His Spirit coming inside of a person's body is a supernatural experience that cannot be obtained with their money, education, or worldly possessions. Through His grace He made a way for this amazing event to take place. The Word tells us, *"For the promise is unto you, and to your children, and to all that are afar off, even as many as the Lord our God shall call" (Acts 2:39).* An individual ought to diligently seek to receive His Spirit.

If a human being were dying, yet, they unquestionably asked for forgiveness, and received Jesus as his or her personal Saviour minutes maybe even seconds before their death, they would be saved. At that point their eternal security would be His greatest concern. *"O the depth of the riches both of the wisdom and knowledge of God! how unsearchable are his judgments, and his ways past finding out" (Romans 11:33)!*

The Lord wants His Spirit to live inside of each individual. The Holy Ghost will give power to every person that receives Him, and authority to overcome sin. Hallelujah! Hallelujah! Hallelujah! Never ending praise and endless glory belongs to the Only Living God. Hall!

Receive the Holy Ghost in the name of Jesus!

*And it shall come to pass in the last days
saith God, I will pour out of my Spirit upon
all flesh: and your sons and your daughters shall
prophesy, and your young men shall see visions,
and your old men shall dream dreams." And on my
servants and on my handmaidens I will pour out
in those days of my Spirit; and they shall prophesy.*

Acts 2:17-18

Receive deliverance
(from sin and its penalty) and power!

> *Whosoever therefore shall be ashamed of me*
> *and my words in this adulterous and sinful*
> *generation; of him also shall the Son of Man*
> *be ashamed, when he cometh in the*
> *glory of his Father with the holy angels.*

St. Mark 8:38

Jesus is the Saviour of the world.

I dynamically changed after I surrendered my life to Jesus. The Lord wanted me to tell family members and friends about His great salvation plan. In the beginning, a number of them would not receive those eternal life saving words. Nevertheless, they needed to know this good news. Jesus longed to deliver them from their wrong way of living.

A very close friend got upset with me one day while we were talking. She asked if I could talk about something other than Jesus. Lesia could not comprehend the change that took place in me. Before those things happened the two of us got high, drank liquor, and went to many worldly and unholy celebrations. Our lives were being directed by the powers of darkness.

A great aspiration was now growing inside of my heart and mind to be obedient to God's Word; I wanted to do things, which exalted Him. The biblical truths that He began to reveal to me could not be hidden, so with great passion and excitement my desire was to witness to every person who would listen. They needed to know Jesus is a loving and faithful God; His ultimate longing is to save each individual.

Something extremely out of the ordinary had taken place. Fleshly and profaned yearnings no longer controlled my life. It is mind boggling to know God's Spirit lives in me; I have been transformed into a new creature. Through His Word and the mighty power of the Holy Ghost I am learning how to be a virtuous woman who has a new walk, a new talk, and a new way to live my life unto His awesome glory.

I have been altered from being a servant of sin to a child of the Only Living God. Some of the people that could not grasp the changes, which took place in me, have also been saved. They have been converted; sin no longer confines their lives. Jesus is leading and keeping them by His mighty influence. Our desire is to be transformed into His image. We will one day see Jesus (face to face) and live with Him throughout eternity.

For I am not ashamed of the gospel of Christ: for it is the power of God unto salvation to every one that believeth; to the Jew first, and also to the Greek.

Romans 1:16

Receive deliverance
(from sin and its penalty) and power!

*Come unto me, all ye that labour
and are heavy laden, and I will give
you rest. Take my yoke upon you, and
learn of me; for I am meek and
lowly in heart: and ye shall find rest
unto your souls. For my yoke is
easy, and may burden is light.*

Matthew 11:28-30

Jesus is the Only Living God, the King of all kings, and the Lord of all lords.

Jesus longs to deliver and restore each sinner, while there is an opportunity. It is written, *"And Jesus answering said unto them, they that are whole need not a physician; but they that are sick. I came not to call the righteous, but sinners to repentance" (Luke 5:31-32).* As an outcome to their sinful natures, nonbelievers cannot accomplish the exploits He wants them to achieve. His desire is to draw every person out of sin, the amount of offenses they committed does not matter. The Lord wants His Spirit to dwell inside of each individual. He longs to have fellowship with mankind now and throughout eternity.

"But without faith it is impossible to please him: for he that cometh to God must believe that he is, and that he is a rewarder of them that diligently seek him (Hebrews 11:6). Every seeker need to believe that God made a way for this supernatural rebirth to take place. Repentance is

an extremely vital factor in His salvation plan. God's great love will lead people to become godly sorrowful. *Acts 3:19* states, *"Repent ye therefore, and be converted, that your sins may be blotted out, when the times of refreshing shall come from the presence of the Lord."*

It is impossible for an individual to live on both sides of the fence, saved and unsaved. Always remember that Jesus knows all things, never compromise with the devil. A person is a servant of God or a disciple of Satan, there is not an in between place.

God longs for His children to live righteous lives twenty four hours out of every day, three hundred and sixty five days out of each year. Their responsibility is to be obedient (through the assistance of the Holy Ghost) to the things, which are pertaining to His Word. The way individuals represent Jesus is very important. The saints have been given the ability to live their lives in a manner that agrees to His holy standards.

Born again believers will at times make unwise choices to sin, as an effect to their righteous inner man they will become godly sorrowful for his or her wrong doings, turning to God for restoration. Jesus made a way for them to escape the final consequence for sin. *"Even as David also describeth the blessedness of the man, unto whom God imputeth righteousness without works. Saying, blessed are they whose iniquities are forgiven, and whose sins are covered" (Romans 4:6-7).*

> *And the lord said unto the servant, Go out into the highways and hedges, and compel them to come in, that my house may be filled.*
>
> *Luke 14:23*

Receive deliverance (from sin and its penalty) and power!

But we all, with open face beholding
as in a glass the glory of the Lord, are
changed into the same image from glory to
glory, even as by the Spirit of the Lord.

2 Corinthians 3:18

Exaltation, praise, and thanksgivings belong to Jesus Christ; He is the only source of eternal salvation.

Jesus chose me to live my life in a demeanor, which would always express glory and honor to Him. Nevertheless, there was a time I enjoyed going to parties, getting high, drinking, and every other immoral action that the devil led me to do. The Word profoundly proclaims, *"Know ye not, that to whom ye yield yourselves servants to obey, his servants ye are to whom ye obey; whether of sin unto death, or of obedience unto righteousness? (Romans 6:16)* A great consequence (perpetual death) had to be paid for my sinful life style. Discretion was not being used by me; in regards to the actions I enjoyed and longed to do.

Stan and I started getting high together at the age of fifth teen. The two of us were extremely young, and made many wrong decisions that had devastating outcomes. Trying to satisfy him in the manner I did gave him control in our relationship. A deep and misleading love developed within my heart for Stan, deceiving powers dwelled inside those emotions that led me not to think about the critical results of my choices.

Stan and I were children attempting to be adults. The two of us chose to live our lives in a way that was unpleasing to God. When we were younger he tried to fight me, what he didn't know was, I fought back. Two people fighting each other in a relationship could be extremely dangerous. Many hurtful words were said over the years of this unholy union.

Jesus began to express disapproval in regards to the manner I chose to live. He wanted me to know my salvation was extremely important, nothing else mattered. Awareness to God's demands began to be exposed to me by the mighty power of the Holy Ghost. Actions I found satisfying in the beginning were now being revealed to be sinful deeds.

A strong conviction came from within. The corrupt exploits, which at one time fulfilled my fleshly longings, were becoming very difficult for me to perform. A choice had to be made, between God or the devil, righteousness or sin, good or evil. I decided to totally surrender my life to Jesus Christ. A few months later He filled me with the Holy Ghost.

It is by the grace (favor) of God that a person can be saved. Salvation cannot be obtained any other way. There is not a human being who is commendable enough to deserve God's delivering power. *"For by grace are ye saved through faith, and that not of yourselves: it is the gift of God: Not of works, lest any man should boast" (Ephesians 2:8-9).*

In the beginning wherever the devil told me to go, I went. Likewise whatever he told me to do, I did. However, at this time, I want to fight a good fight of faith, and always have my confidence focused entirely in Jesus Christ and the victory He received at Calvary. In addition to the many benefits which were extended to me because of that great triumph.

In the past Stan and I said many unkind words to each other. My desire now is to speak out words that bless his life. The two of us committed fornication with each other any time we desired. As a result to us being married we make love and our bed is not defiled before God. There were periods I lied about small issues trying to make sure he did not get angry. In this chapter of our lives my desire is to tell him the truth about everything, knowing the knowledge of the truth shall make a person free. The Lord has made many changes in our lives.

Suffering was experienced in so many wrong ways because of my foolish and disobedient choices. The afflictions that are now being endured are for Christ's sake unto His awesome glory. Stan will one day become the man God desires him to be. Jesus will empower him for such a time as this, to do great and mighty actions through the power of His Spirit.

When Stan acted inconsiderate to me, there was a fervent longing within that wanted to stand up for my rights. Those unwise reactions did not solve our problems. A wife truly submitting to her husband, giving up her agendas and feelings of being right may sound extreme and unfair. The evidence to those actions being performed has been proven to be very successful. At this point in our marriage I refuse to be influenced by the wrong emotions. The most important concern to me is my husband's salvation.

I ask the Lord to help me to live a holy and righteous life before my children. With His assistance they will be brought up in a manner that is pleasing to Him. God will assist Jason, Whitney, and Stanley Jr. to successfully accomplishing the purposes He has chosen them to achieve. Jesus will help my children to have great confidence in

Him. Regardless to the wrong choices Jason, Whitney, and Stanley Jr. are going to make before they surrender to the Only Living God.

Every child of God is waiting for the last transformation. Jesus promise that He would change our immoral bodies, as a result to His mighty power they will be fashioned like His glorious body. According to the Lord's powerful supernatural influence, He is able to subdue all things unto Himself. At the **Judgement Set of Christ**, He will say, *"Will done my good and faithful servant come into my rest."* All praise and honor belong to Jesus Christ the Saviour of the world!

> *For the Lord himself shall descend*
> *from heaven with a shout, with the*
> *the voice of the archangel, and with the*
> *trump of God: and the dead in Christ*
> *shall rise first: Then we which are alive*
> *and remain shall be caught up together*
> *with them in the clouds, to meet the Lord in*
> *the air: and so shall we ever be with the Lord.*

> *1 Thessalonians 4:16-17*

*P*eace I leave with you, my peace I give unto you:
not as the world giveth, give I unto you. Let not
your heart be troubled, neither let it be afraid. These
things I have spoken unto you, that in me ye might have
peace. In the world ye shall have tribulation:
but be of good cheer; I have overcome the world.

St. John 14:27, 16:33

Chapter 3

Peace

> *Have not I commanded thee? Be strong*
> *and of good courage; be not afraid, neither*
> *be thou dismayed: for the LORD thy*
> *God is with thee whitersoever thou goest.*

> *Joshua 1:9*

Praise and glory belong to Jesus; He is the God of Peace. The Lord does not want anyone to be imprisoned by fear; He longs to give each person a peace that is beyond their understanding.

Every individual have experienced fear in some manner, it is controlled by the power of darkness. We battle to overcome fear each day. The first time it manifested was after Adam sinned. ***"And he said, I heard thy voice in the garden, and I was afraid, because I was naked; and I hid myself" Genesis 3:10.*** It has attempted to overwhelm the human race since that day, and will try to devastate them until the end of this time frame. People who are being controlled by fear do not completely trust Jesus.

Fear is one of Satan's greatest weapons. It was designed to stop the power of God from ruling in people's lives. The devil puts false and fearful thoughts inside of individuals' minds longing for them to meditate on those deliberations. He wants each person to feel unstable because of untrue contemplations. His lies make people question God's Word, which creates fear that develops into doubt.

Fear's strategy is to open entrances for untrue and frightening thoughts to mentally paralyze entities' minds. The devil's objective is to control individual's lives through false deliberations. It will attempt to hinder or even stop them from achieving actions they were created to accomplish. Fearful thoughts must be casted down in the name of Jesus. *2 Corinthians 10:4-5* profoundly states, *"(For the weapons of our warfare are not carnal, but mighty through God to the pulling down of strong holds;) casting down imaginations, and every high thing that exalteth itself against the knowledge of God, and bring into captivity every thought to the obedience of Christ."* Without compromising we must command our thoughts to be controlled by the obedience of the Anointed One Jesus.

Believers having confidence in God's Word will help them to overcome fear. The Lord wants his children to unquestionably believe the things He promised. *"(For we walk by faith, not by sight;)" (2 Corinthians 5:7).* When people meditate on fearful thoughts their actions are stopping faith from manifesting. Always remember, faith will terminate fear every time it is exploited to the glory of God.

Each saint must become more skillful relating to the scriptures, there are many bible verses that will (in a process of time), stop fear. They should study and mediate on God's Word, casting down every negative and unproductive thought, taking authority over those deliberations in the name of Jesus. The Lord longs to deliver each person from fear. When individuals have confidence in Him; He will work mightily on their behalf.

God promised that He would protect His children; we should trust Him, and make an unwavering decision not to fear. His Word tells us, *"Surely he shall deliver thee from the snare of the fowler, and from the noisome pestilence. He shall cover thee with his feathers, and under his wings shalt thou trust: his truth shall be thy shield and buckler" (Psalm 91:3-4).* Believers should not permit fear to come inside of their minds, regardless to the circumstances that could be taking place around them. *Psalm 91:7* strongly declares, *"A thousand shall fall at thy side, and ten thousand at thy right hand; but it shall not come nigh thee."*

Jesus wants each person to be entrenched in His Love. We must diligently seek to know the fullness of God's great compassion. *"That Christ may dwell in your hearts by faith; that ye, being rooted and grounded in love, May be able to comprehend with all saints what is the breadth, and length, and depth, and height; And to know the love of Christ, which passeth knowledge, that ye might be filled with all the fullness of God" (Ephesians 3:17-19).*

God has an unconditional, unchanging, and undeserved infinite love for every person. *1 John 4:9-10* utters, *"In this was manifested the love of God toward us, because that God sent his only begotten Son into the world, that we might live through him. Herein is love, not that we loved God, but that he loved us, and sent his Son to be the propitiation for our sins."* Jesus wants to teach each saint how to love in an unrestricted manner. As an outcome to that being accomplished fear will not be able to torment them.

Receive the peace of God in the name of Jesus

The LORD is my light and my salvation;
whom shall I fear? The LORD is the strength
of my life; of whom shall I be afraid?

Psalm 27:1-2

Peace

For God hath not given us the spirit of fear; but of power, and of love, and of a sound mind.

2 Timothy 1:7

Jesus is a mind regulator, eternal praise belong to Him.

Unlimited freedom can only be founded in Christ Jesus because who the Son makes free is free indeed. There was a time I could not declare that statement. Many years ago, fear began to overwhelm me, at that phase I was not aware of the apprehension which existed inside of my mind.

Confusing and aggressive thoughts began to mentally paralyze me. The intimidating deliberations and perplexing anxieties became more intense, and they continuously bombarded my mind. I prayed, fasted, and studied God's Word, trying to receive deliverance; nevertheless, it did not appear to be a strategy that would bring me complete liberty.

A few people were told the things that were occurring, as an effect to their responses, I believe no other person had ever experienced this type of psychological trial. Hopelessness remained hidden within me, my mind felt like a time bomb which was getting ready to explode! Yet, no one perceived the mental conflicts that were taking place,

The devil discerned I cared too much about other people's opinions.

Be extremely cautious concerning the things you allow him to perceive about you. *Ephesians 4:27* tells us, *"Never give place to the devil."* Doubtful and nervous reactions opened a door for him to forcefully disturb me.

A number of friends came against me; I did not understand their unkind actions. It has always been my desire to be a nice and loving person. Nothing was done by me that should have changed their attitudes to such a degree. Although they saw the conversion, which took place, I no longer desired to do the sinful actions we at one time did together. My new lifestyle convicted them of their wrong way of living.

I finally realized Satan controlled the fear that made me feel so mentally exhausted and unstable. Focusing on his lies instead of God's Word was unwise. The demonic influence of that captivity led me to isolate myself. When He tells us, *"No weapon that is formed against thee shall prosper; and every tongue that shall rise against thee in judgment thou shall condemn. This is the heritage of the servants of the Lord and their righteousness is of me saith the Lord" (Isaiah 54:17).* My help and total freedom was entirely in Jesus.

The mental oppression became so strong; I did not have any peace. Whitney and Stanley Jr. longed to go outside to play but they were too young to be outside without supervision. Our door way entrance was as far as I went. Fear had taken control over my life. A profound captivity had imprisoned me and it did not appear to be a way to escape.

Nothing had been said to my husband concerning the demonic assaults, which were disturbing my frame of mind. Self absorbed feelings of embarrassment consumed me that made it even more distressing. One day while we were outside I tried to go back into our house in an extreme way. When Stan saw those things happening he discerned something was wrong. However, he could not identify with the amount of fear that had my thoughts under a forceful attack.

I finally realized my thoughts and every other thing had to be surrendered to Jesus. *James 4:7* tells us, *"Submit yourselves therefore to God. Resist the devil, and he will flee from you."* Over a period of time the psychological assaults began to stop. A great peace came inside of me. His Word tells us, *"Thou wilt keep him in perfect peace, whose mind is stayed on thee: because he trusteth in thee" (Isaiah 26:3).* After the oppression stop, I was no longer concerned about a person's opinions. The Lord wanted me to meditate on His undeserved love, goodness, and faithfulness. It is written, *"Thou shalt not bow down thyself to them, nor serve them: for I the Lord thy God am a jealous God" (Exodus 20:5).* Only the things, which are done unto His glory, will make a difference at the end!

At the conclusion of this test, I accepted the fact that people did have a right to be friendly or unkind to me. Though sadness, intimidation, or any other bad emotions will not be permitted to disturbed or confuse my mind. God has given me a responsibility to love, forgive, and pray for every person. The Word tells us, *"Beloved, let us love one another: for love is of God; and everyone that loveth is born of God, and knoweth God. He that loveth not knoweth not God; for God is love" (1 John 4:7-8).*

"There is no fear in love; but perfect love casteth out fear; because fear hath torment. He that feareth is not made perfect in love" (1 John 4:18). We should try our best (with the assistance of the Holy Ghost) to become perfect in God's love. Each person ought to live their lives

in a method, which will always reveal His compassionate affections. He gave every believer a great accountability to love, regardless to the manner in which they are mistreated, wrongfully used, or disregarded. *"And above all things have fervent charity among yourselves: for charity shall cover the multitude of sins" (1 Peter 4:8).* **Jesus' love covered the sins of the world!**

> *Fear thou not; for I am with thee: be not dismayed; for I am thy God: I will strengthen thee; yea, I will help thee; yea, I will uphold thee with the right hand of my righteousness. Behold, all they that were incensed against thee shall be ashamed and confounded: they shall be as nothing; and they that strive with thee shall perish. For I the LORD thy God will hold thy right hand, saying unto thee, fear not; I will help thee.*
>
> *Isaiah 41:10-11, 13*

Peace

Fear is false evidence that appear to be real. There was a time that I would not deal with fear, regardless to how overwhelmed and confuse it made me fill. I had just surrendered to Jesus and He had so many plans. The devil perceived and He did not want me to stand. Satan used fear as a tool, and O what a fight, he bombarded my mind with fearful thoughts day and night. At that time I felt so alone. I had so how moved out of my comfort zone.

This inward prison became extremely difficult to hid, peace and safety I felt at home I no longer wanted to go outside. Those difficulties were very hard to share; my thoughts told me that no one would care. Stan finally realized fear was badly disturbing my mind, at that point I was already confined. My children were no longer correctly covered, because of an issue that tormented their mother. For many years I did not know why I had to go though, it was a difficult test that I am now able to share with you.

I was granted God's grace which helped me to endure the race. He gave me peace and for a while my problems ceased. The Lord wanted me to trust Him with all my heart so the right relationship with Him would start. I now know Jesus will give me victory in every situation that is one of the benefits to His great salvation.

The Lord laid down His life at Calvary; He made a way for me to be made free, and live with Him throughout eternity. Everything will be at its best, when He says, *"Well done My good and faithful servant come into My rest!"*

Peace

*Forbearing one another,
and forgiving one another,
if any man have a quarrel
against any: even as Christ
forgave you, so also do ye.*

Colossians 3:13

Unlimited and bountiful praise belongs to Christ Jesus, all majesty and authority is His now and throughout time.

There is a liberating power in forgiving a person. Nevertheless, if an individual makes a wrong choice to be unforgiving a great captivity will develop in their life. Its imprisonment becomes more intense as an outcome to the amount of time it takes for him or her to truly forgive. When a person chooses not to pardon someone, lethal penalties take control, which have the ability to psychologically enslave a rebellious entity. That confinement has the capacity to obtain authority over their thoughts, emotions, decisions, and eternal destiny.

When someone rejects God's command to forgive they are placing their life in a dangerous place. *"For if ye forgive men their trespasses, your heavenly Father will also forgive you. But if ye forgive not men their trespasses, neither will your Father forgive your trespasses" (Matthew 6:14-15).* God wants each person to be able to perform this vital act of mercy. The Lord has given every human being a responsibility to forgive.

A defiant person will not be able to perform the deeds they were chosen to accomplish, it limits or even stops God's power from ruling in their life. A situation should never be judged without using His Word. The way an individual deals with this issue will have a great influence in his or her natural and eternal life (good if they forgive, bad it they won't).

Truly examine yourself, do not wait another day! Unforgiveness is controlled by the authorities of darkness. Satanic powers will attempt to devastate you with confusion, anger, and outbursts of wrath, if you refuse to be merciful. Demonic spirits long to bring animosity, hatred, and such like feelings. Do not permit those things to control you.

I experienced the captivity of being unforgiving. The consequences that came from this great bondage taught me how to forgive people even if they do not ask. However, when those things were taking place unhappiness, uncertainty, and other disturbing feelings came into my mind. Two people did something that was mentally and emotionally injuring to me. One was forgiven; however, I did not exonerate the other person. The individual who was pardoned never asked for forgiveness, though I have sincerely demonstrated compassion to them. There is not any sadness, confusion, or anger in my mind in regards to the actions that took place.

I truly believed I had a rightful choice not to forgive the other person. When those things were happening there was not any perception inside of me which revealed my decision had bad consequences. Over a period of time I realized the other individual had to be forgiven. My freedom was in showing them mercy. The Word of God tells us, **"Blessed are the merciful for they shall obtain mercy" (Matthew 5:7).**

Excitement and joy profoundly grew within me following salvation. I was given a great responsibility to tell people about God's awesome deliverance plan. *Mark 16:15* declares, *"Go ye into all the world, and preach the gospel to every creature."* To my shock I had to witness Jesus' love, forgiveness, and saving grace to someone that deeply offended me. In the beginning witnessing to them did not feel right. However, the Lord had performed so many extraordinary and undeserved deeds of love on every person's behalf. Those astonishing acts of compassion had to be told.

Jesus is so amazing! One night He permitted the person that I finally forgave, and I to see each other at a place they should not have been. While we were talking He gave me peace and the capacity to say, "I forgive you." Only through His great influence could those words be said.

At this period in my life it usually isn't difficult to forgive, however, on the occasions that it might appear to be challenging, God always helps me to make the right decision. The Lord continuously demonstrates Himself to be the greatest forgiver. At Calvary when Jesus said, *"It is finished!"* He made a way for each person's sins (past, present, and future) to be forgiven.

> *And be ye kind one to another,*
> *tenderhearted, forgiving one*
> *another, even as God for Christ's*
> *sake hath forgiven you.*
>
> *Ephesians 4:32*

Peace

*For he shall give his
angles charge over thee, to
keep thee in all thy ways.*

Psalms 91:11

Thanksgivings and praise belongs to God because He guards His children with a mantel of protection.

One day God stated I was connected to Him by the blood covenant of Jesus Christ, which gave me a right to receive His promises. They overflowed to my husband and our children. This was an extremely insightful eye opener, over the years I had learned many of those guarantees. During testimony service on the following Sunday I was not able to completely declare that awesome spiritual revelation. However, those proclamations were still burning inside of my heart and mind.

Jesus wanted to confirm His Words directly to me. To my surprise Pastor Cannon's message was about the covenant and promises of God. The preaching of His guarantees made the statements He previously stated go deeper into my mind. *"For the word of God is quick, and powerful, and sharper than any to twoedged sword, piercing even to the dividing asunder of soul and spirit, and is a discerner of the thoughts and intents of the heart" (Hebrews 4:12).* Unrestricted praise started to come out my mouth.

Satan knows that God longs to reveal Himself to His children. He had to do something to stop this confirmation from being completely comprehended. The devil came to steal, kill, and destroy; as a result to his evil influences I began to have a seizure. Always remember that sickness is controlled by the powers of darkness. After my consciousness returned I started to uncontrollably cry. When this illness is taking place disturbing feelings of sadness and confusion attempts to overwhelm me. Getting sick at church was unbelievable; however, thinking about it now, there is not a better place to be when a demonic attack is taking place.

Mother Cannon declared she had called my husband, at first her words were a little startling. Stan had never come inside our church; it took him about ten minutes to get there. With great concern in his eyes, he walked into the sanctuary. Stan began to ask me questions trying to make sure I was ok.

My husband got an opportunity to meet Pastor Cannon and some of God's people because of a condition, which in the beginning appeared to be life threatening. It looked like something awful had transpired. Nevertheless, *"All things work together for good to them that love God, to them who are the called according to his purpose" (Romans 8:28).*

Cause me to hear thy loving kindness
in the morning; for in thee do I trust: cause
me to know the way wherein I should
walk; for I lift up my soul unto thee.

Psalm 143:8

Peace

But God, who is rich in mercy, for his great love wherewith he loved us. Even when we were dead in sins, hath quickened us together with Christ, (by grace ye are saved). And hath raised us up together, and made us sit together in heavenly places in Christ Jesus.

Ephesians 2:4-6

God's abundant grace and life giving power belong to each individual that will receive it. He is rich in mercy and has a massive love for mankind.

For many years I had a great longing to perform sinful actions. When those things were happening, I did not know that the devil was controlling my life. The Word clearly declares, *"Know ye not, that to whom ye yield yourself servants to obey, his servants ye are to whom ye obey; whether of sin unto death, or of obedience unto righteousness" (Romans 6:16)?* A person is a child of God or a disciple of Satan, righteousness or sin. *"No man can serve two masters: for either he will hate the one, and love the other; or else he will hold to the one, and despise the other. Ye cannot serve God and mammon" (Matthew 6:24).*

The Lord began to deal with me in a wonderful way, my manner of thinking started to change. When I attempted to do immoral exploits feelings of guilt began to condemn me, a strong conviction came from within. As a product to those emotions, I surrendered to Jesus. Through His mighty power a transformation took place. *"For he hath made him to be sin for us, who knew no sin; that we might be made the righteousness of God in him" (2 Corinthians 5:21).* The overwhelming desire to sin no longer controlled my life.

The Messiah made a way for each sinner to receive victory over sin. *"And you hath he quickened, who were dead in trespasses and sins. Wherein time past ye walked according to the course of this world, according to the prince of the power of the air, the spirit that now worketh in the children of disobedience" (Ephesians 2:1-2).* The Lord changes each sinner's (those that will believe and accept Jesus as their Saviour) hopeless destination (for in Adam all die) to a glorious predestination (that only they can change) to obtain eternal life. Through the power of the Holy Ghost, Jesus quickens their mortal bodies.

Jesus has given each believer victory; He made a way for them to be a part of His spiritual family. The exploits that are produced from individuals' having faith in the Lord's triumphant actions, will help them to be obedient to His Word. He wants every person to obtain supernatural and unlimited power, through them receiving His Spirit. *Acts 1:8* tells us, *"But ye shall receive power, after that the Holy Ghost is come upon you: and ye shall be witnesses unto me both in Jerusalem, and in all Judae'-a, and in Sama'-ri-a, and unto the uttermost part of the earth."*

> *Giving thanks unto the Father, which hath made us meet to be partakers of the inheritance of the saints in light. Who hath delivered us from the power of darkness, and hath translated us into the Kingdom of his dear Son. In whom we have redemption through his blood, even the forgiveness of sins.*
>
> *Colossians 1:12-14*

Peace

In him was life; and the life was the light of men. And the light shineth in darkness; and the darkness comprehended it not.

St. John 1:4-5

Jesus is an astonishing light that shines in the midst of darkness.

Years ago our city as well as other cities in Michigan had a black out. A number of cities in various states and parts of Canada also experienced electrical difficulties. This was one of the largest power malfunctions to ever occur. It will go down in history as the day that the lights went out.

People were confused and troubled; the spirit of fear began to overwhelm some of them because no one knew why the electricity had gone out. Individuals were coming to their own conclusions; some proclaimed a Down River Area electrical system had a power shortage. People justified it to be a problem in another state, which supplied electricity to the different locations. There were other wrong assumptions made about the situation that was taking place.

I remembered I did not have any medicine. Stan rushed me to the drug store, however, they were closed. Not being able to receive my medicine could have been dangerous. At this point I had to believe in God's protecting power, He has always proven Himself to be extremely faithful.

The stores, gas stations, restaurants, and just about every other business had to close. It was impossible for them to properly function without electricity. Only a few small stores stayed opened, they used calculators to add up the items being purchased. A great amount of money was lost that day. People rushed to places which sold ice, attempting to keep their food cool.

This unpleasant situation was not too difficult to deal with while it was day. Nevertheless, when it became night a mysterious force developed in the darkness that I had never seen before. The electricity was off; though the Light was not out. *"For God, who commanded the light to shine out of darkness, hath shined in our hearts, to give the light of the knowledge of the glory of God in the face of Jesus Christ" (2 Corinthians 4:6).*

It was extremely dangerous for a person to drive, ride a bike, or walk down the streets. Some people were driving very slowly with their bright lights on. Others walked down the streets caring flashlights. The Word cries out, *"If we say that we have fellowship with him, and walk in darkness, we lie, and do not the truth. But if we walk in the light, as he is in the light, we have fellowship one with another, and the blood of Jesus Christ his Son cleanseth us from all sin" (1 John 1:6-7).*

A countless number of stars were shining so brightly in the sky. It was an astonishing power within the darkness that illuminated them in an incredible way. They looked spectacular and unbelievably beautiful. I was amazed; by the glory of God.

People were outside sitting on their porches. It looked like no one wanted to go inside of their homes. Individuals could not execute actions they normally performed. Things people often enjoyed and at times took for granted were not available.

One of my husband's friends called him; he told Stan they were being evacuated from their neighborhood. A large oil company was having small fires, which could have started a chain reaction of explosions. We could see helicopters flying in that area. If the oil company had exploded many people's lives would have been in great danger, including every person who lived in our neighborhood and surrounding cities.

One of our neighbors also heard about the things that were taking place. They called the police department to see if we needed to evacuate. She stated the police had not received orders declaring an evacuation. My husband and I were thinking about leaving our house, however, after Stan heard the police report he did not feel it was necessary for us to depart.

If it had been an evacuation, so many people would not have known they needed to leave their homes. Those individuals might have ultimately lost their lives, if the oil company had a chain reaction of explosions. Many were still living immorally wrong. On **"Judgment Day"** a great price would have had to be paid for their sinful way of existing. It is written, *"And I saw the dead, small and great, stand before God; and the books were opened: and another book was opened, which is the book of life: and the dead were judged out of those things which were written in the books, according to their works" (Revelation 20:12).*

If a born again believer had died that night, they would one day receive eternal life through Christ Jesus. *"For we know that if our earthly house of this tabernacle were dissolved, we have a building of God, an house not made with hands, eternal in the heavens" (2 Corinthians 5:1). "Not by works of righteousness which we have done, but according to his mercy he saved us, by the washing of regeneration, and renewing of the Holy Ghost. Which he shed on us abundantly through Jesus Christ our Saviour. That being justified by his grace, we should be made heirs according to the hope of eternal life" (Titus 3:5-7).*

The electricity was off for about twenty four hours. We learned how to survive without electrical energy during that length of time. People are not always thankful for the acts of kindness God does on their behalf. That situation occurring helped some individuals to appreciate the wonderful blessings He gives to them.

The Lord wants His peace to be inside of every believer's heart. He tells us, *"Peace I leave with you, my peace I give unto you: not as the world giveth, give I unto you. Let not your heart be troubled, neither let it be afraid" (St John 14:27).* God has empowered His beloved children to have victory in every part of their lives. He is rich in mercy and compassion greatly abounds in Him. Nevertheless, on **"Judgment Day"** He will not demonstrate sympathy to those who would not receive Him as their Saviour. Be sure beyond a shadow of a doubt that you have surrendered yourself to the Only Living God.

How sweet are thy words unto my taste!
Yea, sweeter than honey to my mouth! Thy word is
a lamp unto my feet, and a light unto my path.

Psalm 119:103,105

Peace

Behold, I give unto him my covenant of peace:
And he shall have it, and his seed after him,
even the covenant of an everlasting priesthood;
because he was zealous for his God, and made
an atonement for the children of Israel.

Numbers 25:12-13

Jesus longs to give each person a tranquility that is beyond their understanding; He is Jehovah Shalom the Prince of Peace, all praise and glory belongs to Him. The Lord want His beloved to experience a harmony where there is nothing missing or broken. Jesus' wants to grant us peace spiritually, mentally, physically, and financially. Below are Scriptures about His peace.

"The LORD lift up his countenance upon thee, and give thee peace. And they shall put my name upon the children of Israel; and I will bless them."

Numbers 6:26-27

"I will both lay me down in peace, and sleep: for thou, LORD, only makest me dwell in safety."

Psalm 4:8

"Mark the perfect man, and behold the upright: for the end of that man is peace."

Psalm 37:37

*"O that thou hadst hearkened to my commandments!
Then had thy peace been as a river, and thy righteousness
as the waves of the sea. Thy seed also had been as the
sand, and the offspring of thy bowels like the gravel
thereof; his name should not have been cut off nor
destroyed from before me. There is no peace, saith the
LORD for the wicked."*

Isaiah 48:18-19/22

*"Salt is good: but if the salt have lost his saltness,
wherewith will ye season it? Have salt in yourselves, and
have peace one with another."*

St. Mark 9:50

*"Glory to God in the highest and on earth peace, good will
toward men."*

St. Luke 2:14

*"And into whatsoever house ye enter, first say, Peace be
to this house. And if the son of peace be there, your peace
shall rest upon it: if not, it shall turn to you again."*

St. Luke 10:5-6

*"These things I have spoken unto you, that in me ye might
have peace. In the world ye shall have tribulation: but be
of good cheer; I have overcome the world."*

St. John 16:33

"To all that be in Rome, beloved of God, called to be saints: Grace to you and peace from God our Father, and the Lord Jesus Christ."

Romans 1:7

"THEREFORE being justified by faith, we have peace with God through our Lord Jesus Christ: By whom also we have access by faith into this grace wherein we stand, and rejoice in hope of the glory of God."

Romans 5:1-2

"How then shall they call on him in whom they have not believed? And how shall they believe in him of whom they have not heard? And how shall they hear without a preacher? And how shall they preach, except they be sent? As it is written, HOW BEAUTIFUL ARE THE FEET OF THEM THAT PEARCH THE GOSPEL OF PEACE, AND BRING GLAD TIDING OF GOOD THINGS!"

Romans 10:14-15

"Be perfect, be of good comfort, be of one mind, live in peace; and the God of love and peace shall be with you."

2 Corinthians 13:11

"For in Christ Jesus neither circumcision availeth any thing, nor uncircumcision, but a new creature. And as many as walk according to this rule, peace be on them and mercy, and upon the Israel of God."

Galatians 6:15-16

"But now in Christ Jesus ye who sometimes were far off are made nigh by the blood of Christ. For he is our peace, who hath made both one, and hath broken down the middle wall of partition between us. Having abolished in his flesh the enmity, even the law of commandments contained in ordinances; for to make in himself of twain one new man, so making peace."

Ephesians 2:13-15

"And that he might reconcile both unto God in one body by the cross, having slain the enmity thereby: And came and preached peace to you which were afar off, and to then that were nigh. For through him we both have assess by one Spirit unto the Father."

Ephesians 2:16-18

"Be careful for nothing; but in every thing by prayer and supplication with thanksgiving let your requests be made know unto God. And the peace of God, which passeth all understanding, shall keep your hearts and minds through Christ Jesus."

Philippians 4:6-7

"Forbearing one another, and forgiving one another, if any man have a quarrel against any: even as Christ forgave you, so also do ye. And above all these things put on charity, which is the bond of perfectness. And let the peace of God rule in your hearts, to the which also ye are called in one body; and be ye thankful."

Colossians 3:13-15

"And we beseech you, brethren, to know them which labour among you, and are over you in the Lord, and admonish you: And to esteem them very highly in love for their work's sake. And be at peace among yourselves."

1 Thessalonians 5:12-13

"Now the Lord of peace himself give you peace always by all means. The Lord be with you all. The grace of our Lord Jesus Christ be with you all. A-men."

2 Thessalonians 3:16/18

"Follow peace with all men, and holiness, without which no man shall see the Lord."

Hebrews 12:14

"FOR HE THAT WILL LOVE LIFE, AND SEE GOOD DAYS, LET HIM REFRAIN HIS TONGUE FROM EVIL, AND HIS LIPS THAT THEY SPEAK NO GUILE: LET HIM ESCHEW EVIL, AND DO GOOD; LET HIM SEEK PEACE, AND ENSUE IT." FOR THE EYES OF THE LORD ARE OVER THE RIGHTEOUS, AND HIS EARS ARE OPEN UNTO THEIR PRAYER; BUT THE FACE OF THE LORD IS AGAINST THEM THAT DO EVIL."

1 Peter 3:10-12

Grace and peace be multiplied unto you through the knowledge of God, and of Jesus our Lord. According as his divine power hath given unto us all things that pertain unto life and godliness, through the knowledge of him that hath called us to glory and virtue.

2 Peter 1:2-3

But ye are a chosen generation, a royal
priesthood, an holy nation, a peculiar
people; that ye should shew forth
the praises of him who hath called you
out of darkness into his marvelous light.

1Peter 2:9

Chapter 4

Chosen

In whom also we have obtained an inheritance,
being predestinated according to the purpose
of him who worketh all things after the counsel
of his own will. That we should be to the
praise of his glory, who first trusted in Christ.

Ephesians 1:11

Praise and dominion belong to God; He wants us to trust Him and to walk in His righteousness so we will have a right to receive His unlimited blessings.

I began to seek a place of worship that was closer to my house. God was also directing an elder at Solomon's Temple to start a church. We did not know each other personally, however, he prayed for me a few times. His wife also attended Solomon's Temple though we never met. Our church was large and had many members. Jesus led Elder Lovell and Sister Tina Cannon to a building, which was ten minutes from where I lived. I stopped going to Solomon's Temple, and started to attend True Worship Church. The Lord's presence could be felt the first Sunday I visited. His love and power are allowed to freely move and multiply there.

God sent an enormous light (True Worship Church) to a city where people needed to hear his errorless Word being profoundly preached. TWC has and will continue to have a great influence in that area. Through faith in the finished works Jesus accomplished at Calvary, God's Word being powerfully preached, and prayer, we will do extensive damage to the powers of darkness. His Spirit is permitted to be in control at True Worship Church. He directed me to a spiritual house that is fortified with His mighty power.

Pastor Cannon is submissive to the Spirit of God. Jesus has given him many visions over the years. He also has the capacity to unite himself to other people's spiritual dreams. My pastor is prayerful, proficient in God's Word, and very dedicated to the things he was called to do. He cares about the needs of others, most importantly the welfare of individuals' souls. Pastor Cannon has a great desire to help people with their spiritual and natural needs. The Lord is going to bless him to do extraordinary things through the impressive power of the Holy Ghost.

Jesus has spoken many words of encouragement and instructions to me through Pastor Cannon's preaching and teaching. He permits the fruit of the Spirit to manifest inside of him. His godly example teaches our congregation how to have faith in Jesus Christ, to extend love to people, be forgiving, and many other things. He acknowledges his shortcomings and at times unwise choices. Pastor Cannon loves Jesus, his wife, their children, and people in general. One day he will receive a crown of life.

First Lady Tina Cannon is a loving and concerned person. She has been a blessing to me as well as a vast number of people. There were Sundays in which my children and I were not able to attend service. At those phases she would call me. Lady Tina Cannon stated that we were loved and missed, her acts of kindness made a difference in my life. Our First Lady tries very hard to be obedient to the things she was chosen to successfully achieve. As a result of her obedience, Jesus will one day reward her.

Jesus blessed True Worship Church with many people. He wants them to be bright lights that will draw sinners out of sin into His righteous. Through the mighty power of God's Spirit, each believer will live successful lives. The children at our church are being trained by anointed preaching, the teaching of God's Word, and our examples. At the Judgment Seat of Christ, He will bless those men, women, and children.

Jesus has given each person that surrenders their lives to Him a right to be a part of His glorious church. *"In whom ye also trusted, after that ye heard the word of truth, the gospel of your salvation; in whom also after that ye believed, ye were sealed with the holy Spirit of promise"* *(Ephesians 1:13).* *"For whom he did foreknow, he also did predestinate to be conformed to the image of his Son, that he might be the firstborn among many brethren"* *(Romans 8:29).*

> *Moreover whom he did predestinate, them he also called: and whom he called, them he also justified: and whom he justified, them he also glorified.*
>
> *Romans 8:30*

Chosen

In this was manifested the love of God towards us, because that God sent his only begotten Son into the world, that we might live through him.

1 John 4:9

God is love! He is all powerful, all knowing, and everywhere at the same time.

As an effect of God's great feelings of affection He created the human race. The Lord made an unwavering decision to love each individual. Through God's foresight of the fall of mankind, His vast compassion motived Him to redeem the human race. It is written, **"Forasmuch as ye know that ye were not redeemed with corruptible thing, as silver and gold, from your vain conversation received by tradition from your fathers. But with the precious blood of Christ, as of a lamb without blemish and without spot. Who verily was foreordained before the foundation of the world, but was manifest in these last times for you"** (1 Peter 1:18-20).

There is not a deeper feeling of admiration than the love Jesus has for every person. *St John 15:13* declare, **"Greater love hath no man than this, that a man lay down his life for his friends."** The Lord wants each believer to know the profundity of His great concern.

Herein is love, not that we loved God, but that he loved us, and sent his Son to be the propitiation for our sins" (1 John 4:10).

Jesus does not want people to be discouraged by unproductive thoughts, the difficulties of life, or the power of darkness that will forcefully come against them. They should not be deceived by the way things look or feel because we walk by faith and not by sight. *"For I am persuaded, that neither death, nor life, nor angels, nor principalities, nor powers, nor things present, nor things to come, nor height, nor depth, nor any other creature, shall be able to separate us from the love of God, which is in Christ Jesus our Lord" (Romans 8:38-39).*

The only thing that could separate a person from God's love is them refusing to accept Jesus as their Lord and Saviour! A human being who makes that wrong choice will be judged because of their disobedient decision. *"Jesus saith unto him, I am the way, the truth and the life: no man cometh to the Father, but by me" (John 14:6). "Then shall he say also unto them on the left hand, Depart from me, ye cursed, into everlasting fire, prepared for the devil and his angels. And these shall go away into everlasting punishment" (Matthew 25:41, 46).* This sentence is too great of a price for anyone to be willing to pay as a final outcome of their wrong way of living.

"God shall wipe away all tears from their eyes; and there shall be no more death, neither sorrow, nor crying, neither shall there be pain; for the former things are passed away" (Revelation 21:4). This scripture declares there won't be any tears in heaven. If it were, Jesus would weep throughout eternity, as a result of the great consequences each person would receive that did not accept Him as their Saviour.

Hereby perceive we the love of God,
because He laid down his life for us.

1 John 3:16

Chosen

*A*nd whatsoever ye do in word or deed,
do all in the name of the Lord Jesus, giving
thanks to God and the Father by him.

Colossians 3:17

Jesus Christ is a faithful God. I will bless His name at all times and His praise shall continuously be in my mouth.

The Lord blessed me with a job as a crossing guard. One of my duties was to assist the middle and high school students across an extremely busy street, the most dangerous street in our city. In the beginning this job was difficult to do, I had to observe five traffic lights, cars coming from five directions, and students that were going or coming from each school.

Snow or ice covered the ground for more than a month. My job required me to stand outside for about two and a half hours a day, Monday through Friday. When I had to walk to work, and back home another hour and a half was added. Before going to bed my thoughts would be centered on how much I dreaded doing that job. Many mornings those unproductive thoughts led me to stay at home.

A strong conviction came within me because of my bad work habits. I stopped meditating on those negative feeling, after having that thought. My responsibility was to proficiently carry out deeds that appeared to be small and insignificant. I had to learn how to perform duties in a manner that established a dependable character.

On the spiritual side my responsibility was to be a blessing and guide to every person who walked pass. Jesus wanted me to declare His gospel to each individual. Most of the people I talked to did not know they needed to be delivered from their wrong way of living. He led me to give out tracks (leaflets) which declared His great salvation plan. The Lord longed for every person to know the gospel has massive and astonishing powers. The directions of eternal life were revealed in each track.

Doing the spiritual part of this job was not a problem. I believed when it got warmer, I would witness Jesus' great love to a larger number of people. Every individual that submits to the Lord is going to be presented to Him as an extraordinary reward, at the **Judgment Set of Christ.**

And I looked, and behold a white cloud, and upon the cloud one sat like unto the Son of man, having on his head a golden crown, and in his hand a sharp sickle. And another angel came out of the temple, crying with a loud voice to him that sat on the cloud, Thrust in thy sickle, and reap; for the time is come for thee to reap; for the harvest of the earth is ripe.

Revelation 14:14-15

Chosen

Trust in the LORD and do good; so shalt thou dwell in the land, and verily thou shalt be fed.

Psalm 37:3

The Lord is the same yesterday, today, and forever.

God has endowed me with a content spirit that helps me to stand on His Word and be unmovable. I am learning how to have confidence in Him while going through objectionable situations. My hope and insurance is in the Lord, every Word that He declared will come to pass.

Jesus gave me a great longing to write books, there are not any payments until the first manuscript is completed. He has supplied every need that was required over the many years it took for this book to be finished. The Lord placed His undeserved and endless favor upon my life. The Word says, *"But thou shalt remember the LORD thy God: for it is he that giveth thee power to get wealth, that he may establish his covenant which he sware unto thy fathers, as it is this day" (Deuteronomy 8:18).*

One day Jesus is going to forcefully open doors for me, which no man can shut. He will furthermore keep entrances closed that the powers of darkness are behind. The controller of those evil forces does not want the Lord's purposes to be fulfilled. **Nevertheless, if God is for me, who is the world against me!**

There shall no evil befall thee, neither shall any plague come nigh thy dwelling. For he shall give his angels charges over thee, to keep thee in all thy ways.

Psalm 91:10-11

Chosen

*Go ye into all the world, and preach
the gospel to every creature.*

(Mark 16:15)

The privilege of being a worker in Jesus' great harvest has been granted to you, for the harvest is ripe but the labors are few. He wants to give every person eternal life that's why He was willing to paid that enormous price. We must study God's Word, pray, and fast, and as a result our purpose for life will come to pass. Each saint has been given a great command. We must go out and bring in every person that we can.

Along with preaching, teaching, and singing of great praise songs, we must also witness to people that feel at church they don't belong because of their wrong. They must be told Jesus paid the price for every person's sinful deeds when His blood was shed at Calvary.

"Always remember through My Spirit I grabbed your hand, however, someone else was sent to reveal My great salvation plan. A night is coming when no man can work, yet, while it is day bring unto Me all who hurt."

On the day of the Lord's, His rewards will be in His hands and He longs to give them to every person that he can. However, our works are going to determine the rewards we will receive. Make sure you have done something to fulfill another person's needs.

*Go ye therefore, and teach all nations,
baptizing them in the name of the Father,
and of the Son, and of the Holy Ghost.*

(Matthew 28:19)

VICKIE CAMPBELL

Chosen

*But the fruit of the Spirit is love, joy, peace,
longsuffering, gentleness, goodness, faith, meekness
temperance; against such there is no law.*

Galatians 5:22

Praise and glory, power and dominion belong to Jesus Christ. He wants the fruit of the Spirit to dwell inside of every individual's heart.

One day I was asked to speak about the fruit of temperance, temperance is to be self controlled. Without God's assistance this action could be impossible to accomplish. He wants each person to have an upright attitude. Believers should always walk in the Spirit so they will not fulfill the lustful longings that are in their flesh. **Romans 12:2** tells us, *"And be not conformed to this world: but be ye transformed by the renewing of your mind, that ye may prove what is that good, and acceptable, and perfect, will of God."*

For self-control to manifest and rule inside of each saint's lives, we are going to have to be tempted by the tempter (Satan). Through our tests and trials we should develop, Christ influenced character, not temperamental or explosive mind frames. *"And not only so, but we glory in tribulations also: knowing that tribulation worketh patience. And patience, experience; and experience, hope: and hope maketh not ashamed; because the love of God is shed abroad in our hearts by the Holy Ghost, which is given to us" Romans 5:3-5* God's Spirit, His Word, and prayer will enlighten us to the things we ought to say, do, or stop doing!

The saints have been given a great responsibility to demonstrate Christ like personalities; only through the power of His Spirit can this action be effectively achieved. He wants to be in control of every area of our lives. We must truly judge ourselves, and make sure we are not argumentative, quick-tempered, offensive, and so on. Every believer has a duty to bind and cast down unproductive thoughts and feelings, we should not permit ourselves to be driven by the wrong emotions.

An individual should never allow a longing to exist inside of them that wants to be confirmed the person who was right in a disagreement. Do not permit a difference of opinions to make division in the body of Christ. We have been chosen to be the representatives of **"God's Divine Kingdom"** our characters are extremely important. He has personally selected us to be ambassadors of His righteousness. Saints' have a great objective to successfully witness the gospel. However, if our tempers are out of control this could be very hard to do, perhaps impossible.

At bible class one night, someone walked past me as if I were invisible, and warmly acknowledged the person that was sitting at my left side. At first their actions were disturbing. I began to pray inside of myself inquiring why they acted in such an unkind manner. Not to many seconds later Jesus replied, **"Love, forgive, and pray."** After fighting with upset and confused emotions; I began to submit myself to a Christ like attitude.

A few minutes later Pastor Cannon started to teach the class. He told us what we should do when unpleasant confrontations are taking place. Our pastor said if someone is disrespectful or unfriendly to us, our obligation is to love, forgive, and pray for them. Pastor Cannon did not know about the situation, which took place. Nor could he perceive Jesus used him to confirm the words He had declared to me.

Praise and appreciation belongs to God because I did not make a wrong decision to become angry, offended, or intimidated. Jesus is teaching me how to deal with people that act unkind. My accountability is to love, forgive, and pray for them. Through the massive actions He accomplished on my behalf, the awesome power of His Spirit, and the difficulties in which I have experienced, He is equipping me to become more like Him.

Blessed is the man that endureth temptation:
for when he is tried, he shall receive the crown of life,
which the Lord hath promised to them that love him.

James 1:12

And I heard a great voice out of heaven saying, Behold, the tabernacle of God is with men, and he will dwell with them, and they shall be his people, and God himself shall be with them, and be their God. And God shall wipe away all tears from their eyes; and there shall be no more death, neither sorrow, nor crying, neither shall there be any more pain: for the former things are passed away. And he that sat upon the throne said, Behold, I make all things new. And he said unto me. Write: for these words are true and faithful. And he said unto me, It is done. I am Alpha and Omega, the beginning and the end. I will give unto him that is athirst of the fountain of the water of life freely.

Revelation 21:3-6

Chapter 5

Revelation

*Thou believest that there is
one God; thou doest well: the
devils also believe, and tremble."*

James 2:19

Praise and honor belong to Christ Jesus; He ordained every authority that exists. Satan is a small tool that Jesus will exploit to reveal His astonishing power.

The devil is the father of all lies, and it is impossible for him to tell the truth. He wants to mislead mankind to eternal destruction, do not believe any of his lying words. Be very cautious, the prince of this world is extremely deceitful. Satan can deceptively appear to be an angle of light. He is consumed by evil.

As an effect of Jesus defeating the devil at Calvary, forms of deception are the only powers that he can use to deceive mankind. He is trying his best to perpetually obliterate every person. Satan has to submit to the conquering actions Jesus profoundly performed on the Cross, the Word of God, and the triumphant authority of the Holy Ghost. Though, he does not want mankind to understand or to effectively use those massive supernatural powers.

At one time the devil was an angel, and his name was Lucifer. God created him perfect. As an outcome of his splendor he was filled with pride. He said, *"I will ascend into heaven, I will exalt my throne above the stars of God: I will sit also upon the mount of the congregation, in the sides of the north: I will ascend above the heights of the clouds; I will be like the most High" (Isaiah 14:13-14).* Lucifer was an archangel, and he had great power. *Ezekiel 28:14-15* declares, *"Thou are the anointed cherub that coverth; and I have set thee so: thou wast upon the holy mountain of God; thou hast walked up and down in the midst of stone and fire. Thou wast perfect in thy ways from the day that thou wast created, till iniquity was found in you."*

Instead of Lucifer doing the actions God created him to perform; he was consumed with extreme arrogance. It is written, *"By the multitude of thy merchandise they have filled the midst of thee with violence, and thou hast sinned: therefore I will cast thee as profane out of the mountain of God: and I will destroy thee, O covering cherub, from the midst of the stones of fire. Thine heart was lifted up because of thy beauty, thou hast corrupted thy wisdom as a reason of thy brightness: I will cast thee to the ground, I will lay you before kings, that they may behold thee" (Ezekiel 28:16-17).*

The devil also influenced a third of God's angels to turn against Him. The King of eternal life could not permit Lucifer's evil influences to continue, he was making division in the firmaments. At an appointed time, God threw him out of heaven. The Word declares, *"How art thou fallen from heaven, O Lu-ci-fer, son of the morning! How art thou cut down to the ground, which didst weaken the nations" (Isaiah 14:12)!* He fell upon the earth, and it was without form and void; and darkness came upon the face of the earth.

Satan knows there is a righteous, holy, and powerful God. He can also perceive he does not have much time remaining. One day the devil will be placed in the **"Lake of Fire"** which was prepared for him and his angels. Satan can sense his days of eternal torment are soon to come. *"And the devil that deceived them was cast into the lake of fire and brimstone, where the beast and the false prophet are, and shall be tormented day and night forever and ever" (Revelation 20:10).*

> *Submit yourselves therefore to God.*
> *Resist the devil, and he will flee from you.*
>
> *James 4:7*

Revelation

*And who is he that will harm you, if ye
be followers of that which is good? But
and if ye suffer for righteousness' sake,
happy are ye: AND BE NOT AFRAID OF
THEIR TERROR, NEITHER BE TROUBLED.*

1 Peter 3:13-14

Continuous praise and honor without ending belong to God now and forever.

God took off his royal deity and revealed himself in the form of a servant, in the body of our Lord and Saviour Jesus Christ. **EL OLHIM (THE EVERLASTING GOD)** putting on the likeness of a man confirmed and demonstrated His willingness to suffer. **EL SHADDAI (ALL SUFFICENT OR ALL MIGHTY)** becoming vulnerable to the limitations of the earth when He is omnipotent (all powerful), omniscience (all knowing), and omnipresent (everywhere at the same time) was another great act of agony.

Jesus faithfully performed each requirement, which were demanded paid the price of sin, and broke the power sin had on every person that would believe. *"For when we were yet without strength, in due time Christ died for the ungodly" (Romans 5:6).* *"But not as the offence, so also is the free gift. For if through the offence of one many be dead, much more the grace of God, and the gift by grace, which is by one man, Jesus Christ, hath abounded unto many" (Romans 5:15).* The actions He achieved put mankind back in the right standings with God.

Before Jesus' death, sin had authority over every person's natural and perpetual life. For the wages of sin is death. On **"Judgment Day"** each individual would have been judged (for their wrong deeds), and eternally separated from a holy and loving God!

Believers should not suffer in the manner in which unbelievers do. Jesus gave them many spiritual devices (faith in the victory that He received at Calvary, prayer, the Word, and the mighty power of the

Holy Ghost) to use. Christians suffer because they refuse to be obedient to the god of this world. Neither will they permit themselves to be controlled or driven by the pride of life, lust of the eyes, or the lust of the flesh.

God wants to teach us how to undergo the difficulties of life unto his excellent greatness. He will exploit suffering to bring people closer to Him. The Word boldly states, *"If we suffer, we shall also reign with him: if we deny him, he also will deny us" (2 Timothy 2:12).* Jesus profoundly declared to Paul the apostle, *"My grace is sufficient for thee: for my strength is made perfect in weakness."* Apostle Paul's response was, *"Most gladly therefore will I rather glory in my infirmities, that the power of Christ may rest upon me" (2 Corinthians 12:9-10).*

Each believer should be prepared to suffer because they esteem the love of God far greater riches than wealth, influential power, or any other thing. *2 Corinthians 5:9-10* insightfully declares, *"Wherefore we labor that whether present or absent we may be accepted of Him. For we must all appear before the judgment seat of Christ; that every one may receive the things done in his body, whether it be good or bad."* We must endure until the end!

If ye be reproached for the name of Christ, happy are ye; for the Spirit of glory and of God resteth upon you: on their part he is evil spoken of, but on your part he is glorified.

1 Peter 4:14

Revelation

For the word of God is quick, and powerful,
and sharper than any twoedged sword, piercing
even to the dividing asunder of soul and spirit,
and of the joints and marrow, and is a discerner
of the thoughts and intents of the heart.

Hebrews 4:12

Before the zigzag lighting cross the multitudes of the sky, Jesus was God. Total praise and glory belongs to Him now and until the end of time. He is the Creator of all things, and without Him nothing was made.

In the beginning God gave all dominion pertaining to the earth to mankind. It is written, *"And God said, Let us make man in our image, after our likeness: and let them have dominion over the fish of the sea, and over the fowl of the air, and over the cattle, and over all the earth, and over every creeping thing that creepeth upon the earth" (Genesis 1:26).* When He declared those unchangeable terms He took all rights and authority from Himself, and every other spiritual life form. The manner in which a person chooses to live determines who will (God or the devil) rule their life.

Ephesians 6:12 tells us, *"For we wrestle not against flesh and blood, but against principalities, against powers, against the rulers of the darkness of this world, against spiritual wickedness in high places."* Every day and night the devil gives his demonic demons assignments to execute destructive actions against each individual. He uses lethal strategies yearning to eliminate the human race. Satan wants his evil spirit to dwell inside of entities' body. The evil one will also employ people to hurt and overwhelm each other. Never permit him to use you to perform his corrupt deeds.

A spiritual confrontation is taking place that **"cannot"** be fought with a person's natural abilities, the battle starts in their mind. Each believer must have confidence in Jesus and the exploits He successfully accomplished; as a product of their faith some will immediately obtain triumph over the mental conflict, others in a process of time. At the conclusion of every battle each believer should receive victory, despite the amount of time it takes for the psychological warfare to end.

Many years ago I had an intense mental conflict. The devil forcefully attacked my mind with false deliberations; he was attempting to drive me crazy. When those things were happening, lying thoughts, confusion, and condemning emotions, tried to devastate me. Over a period of time I began to read **2 Corinthians 10:4-5** it declares, ***"(For the weapons of our warfare are not carnal, but mighty through God to the pulling down of strong holds). Casting down imaginations, and every high thing that exaleth itself against the knowledge of God, and bringing into captivity every thought to the obedience of Christ."***

After repeating **2 Corinthians 10:4-5**, I commanded my mind to be imprisoned by the obedience of the Anointed One Jesus and His anointing. Every thought that was exalting itself against the knowledge of God had to be cast down in the name of Jesus. Contemplations of sickness, death, fear, uncertainty, and such like deliberations could not be permitted to stay in my mind. As time passed complete freedom was received through the mighty delivering power of God. When a person reveals to me that they are experiencing a mental battle, I will advise them to read and study those powerful scriptures.

God wants His children too courageously (through faith, without skepticism) take authority over the powers of darkness. Each saint must proficiently accomplish the actions they were called to do, effectively binding and casting down every evil forces. Our responsibility is to bombard the world with love, prayer, and the Word of God. Faith is a very vital and extremely authoritative tool that must be exploited at all times.

> *Teaching them to observe all things whatsoever I have commanded you: and, lo; I am with you always, even unto the end of the world. A-men'.*
>
> *Matthew 28:20*

Revelation

*"**B**ut all these worketh that one and the self same Spirit, dividing to every man severally as he will. For as the body is one, and hath many members, and all the member of that one body, being many, are one body: so also is Christ."*

1 Corinthians 12:11-12

Jesus is the head of the church. His name has been exalted above every name. At the name of Jesus every knee shall bow and every tongue shall confess that He is Lord to the glory of God.

Through God's Word He gave us an example that explain how the natural body operates. (*1 Corinthians 12:12, 14*) Mankind has always been given natural illustrations to assist them to comprehend spiritual topics. Our body is one and has many members. Likewise the body of Christ is one body (the church) that has an uncountable number of people. (*1Corinthians 12:13*) Each part of our natural body labors together, if one component is weak the other members works harder on behalf of the total body. Their purposes are to make the body live and to function properly. The members of the body of Christ should act in the same manner.

A right handed person does almost everything with that hand, their left hand is not intimidated, neither has it ever attempted to stop the right hand from being productive. An individual's brain is not filled with self importance because it has a great influence over the total body. Neither is a person's heart consumed by pride, as a result to its vital responsibility to pump blood to each member. Those components work together, and are at all times on one accord. Body parts aren't able to function alone for an extensive length of time. Each member performs the task or tasks in which they were designed to do; there has never been any type of division inside the natural body.

The members of the body of Christ have a duty to learn how to operate in the manner that the natural body functions. They should not allow unforgiveness, doubt, fear, or hatred to exist inside of them. This God given organization must not permit division, pride, backbiting, sexual perversions, or any other immoral influences to manifest within it. Those sinful inward activities are deadly assassinator. Their purpose is to weaken, and totally devastate the body of Christ.

Each believer ought to demonstrate a righteous way of living his or her life; their examples will help other people to submit to the Author of eternal salvation. God's desire is to save people. It is written, *"For God so loved the world, that he gave his only begotten Son, that whosoever believeth in him should not perish, but have ever lasting life. For God sent not his Son into the Word to condemn the world; but that the world through him might be saved."* *(St. John 3:16-17).* The saint's purposes are to glorify Him in every situation and to accomplish the actions He wants them to achieve in their lives. As an outcome to those things being done, a vast number of individuals in which no man can number will turn to Jesus, and be delivered from their sinful way of living.

We must pray for the body of Christ, starting with the apostles, prophets, evangelists, pastors, and teachers. Jesus gave them, *"For the perfecting of the saints, for the work of the ministry, for the edifying of the body of Christ"*

(Ephesians 4:12). Jesus selects the fivefold ministry and gives them verbal gifts; their duty is to proclaim the Word of God. Apostles give clear instructions through His Word for the church to follow. Prophets keep people going in the direction that the apostles instituted. At times God will reveal to them things which are going to take place in the future. Evangelists call sinners and the redeemed that have been sidetracked (by the power of darkness) back to God's plan for eternal salvation. Pastors proclaim a message, which feeds and assists people to withstand unto the coming of our Lord and Saviour Jesus Christ. Teachers establish the mind frame of the believers through them teaching God's Word.

Each saint should ask God to strengthen the fivefold ministry with might by His Spirit in the inner man. The apostles, prophets, evangelists, pastors, and teachers need to be blessed spiritually, mentally, physically, and financially. The saint's effective prayers will help them to endure until the end of every confrontation. God is going to empower the fivefold ministry, so they will be able to triumphantly complete the responsibilities of their ministries. He wants His Word to be preached and taught throughout the earth.

The apostles, prophets, evangelists, pastors, and teachers, obligation is to tell people; Jesus gave His life as a sacrifice, and victoriously defeated sin and the devil. They are going to profoundly declare, He did everything that He needed to do on behalf of each person's salvation. The Lord is going to empower those spiritual leaders for such a time as this. They will do extensive damage to the powers of darkness. As an ultimate effect of Jesus' glorious power they will preach and teach God's Word, leading a massive number of people to Him. One day every person that is in the fivefold ministry will receive a crown of life.

Individuals that sing or play musical instruments need prayer, God wants to use their talents. He longs to take us into heavenly places through their gifts. Next to His Word being preached, gospel music is the strongest tool that He employs to draw sinners out of sin. Jesus also encourages the saints through gospel music. We must pray for the people that He chose to execute this great task. Those individuals need wisdom and directions so they won't be deceived by the evil one. Satan wants to mislead them, to use their gifts in a worldly procedure. Every person who have a beautiful voice or plays a musical instrument should exploit their ability or abilities to God's extraordinary glory.

An usher's obligation is to greet and guide every brokenhearted, confused, and fearful sinner, in addition to those who are born again into the sanctuary. They should have a loving and kind spirit, an usher's personality ought to make people feel welcomed and comfortable. When this duty is done in the right manner it will help the seekers to receive God's love, mercy, and delivering power. However, if it is done in the wrong way it could hinder or even stop individuals from being submissive to Jesus. Pray for every usher to perform this responsibility in the right way.

The saints should continuously bind and cast down the powers of darkness in the name of Jesus. We must walk in the authority that He gave to us. The Lord performed each action that He needed to execute, so the members of the body of Christ would always receive victory in every situation that takes place! His Word gives us great hope, it declares, *"Moreover whom he did predestinate, them he also called; and whom he called, them he also justified; and whom he justified, them he also glorified. What shall we then say to these things? If God be for us, who can be against us?" (Romans 8:30-31).*

Each member of the natural body is important. In like manner every person who is a part of the body of Christ is extremely significant to Jesus. He wants to be glorified through the way we choose to live our lives. The saints must declare His unlimited love, endless mercy, and amazing grace!

From whom the whole body fitly joined together and compacted by that which every joint supplieth, according to the effectual working in the measure of every part, maketh increase of the body unto the edifying of itself in love."

Ephesians 4:16

Revelation

*E*YE HATH NOT SEEN, NOR EAR
HEARD, NEITHER HAVE ENTERED
INTO THE HEART OF MAN, THE
THINGS WHICH GOD HATH PREPARED
FOR THEM THAT LOVE HIM.
But God hath revealed them unto us by
His Spirit: for the Spirit searcheth all
things, yea, the deep things of God.

1 Corinthians 2:9-10

Glory, majesty, dominion, and eternal power belong to God.

Jesus wants to give every person that surrenders to Him, the ability to achieve mind-bowling, supernatural, and extraordinary actions. He longs to reveal insightful mysteries to their understanding. *"Even the mystery which hath been hid from ages and from generations, but now is made manifest to his saints. To whom God would make known what is the riches of the glory of this mystery among the Gentiles; which is Christ in you, the hope of glory" (Colossians 1:26-27).* When the Lord gives people His underserved acts of love and kindness those deeds should assist them to trust Him in a greater way. The Anointed One wants each individual to be secure in Him.

When a person is going through difficulties they will at times allow seeds of doubt to be planted in their mind. Doubt is faith's number one enemy. An individual should be extremely careful in regards to the voices they chose to believe. The sound of God's Words, the devil's lying expressions, other people's words, and his or her deliberations (good or bad) will come into their ears and thoughts daily. If a person had strong faith, and believed Jesus to do great and mighty things, however, began to concentrate on doubtful words or contemplations that individual's faith would become weaker. On the other hand, if someone had doubts, nevertheless, they started to listen to words of reassurance their confidence would increase.

The Lord wants us to be able to move (through faith) the mountains of adversities that will attempt to overpower our lives. It is written, *"If ye have faith, and doubt not, ye shall not only do this which is done to the fig tree, but also if ye shall say unto this mountain, Be thou removed, and be thou cast into the sea; it shall be done. And all things, whatsoever ye shall ask in prayer, believing, ye shall receive" (St. Matthew 21-21-22). "But let him ask in faith, nothing wavering. For he that wavereth is like a wave of the sea driven with the wind and tossed" (James 1:6).*

A person having confidence in Jesus should be easy for them to do. The Lord is all powerful there is not anything too hard for Him to accomplish. The Word declares, *"Trust in the LORD with all of thine heart; and lean not unto thine own understanding. In all thy ways acknowledge him, and he shall direct thy paths" (Proverbs 3:5-6).* When an individual choose to be fearful or uncertain, in regards to Jesus' faithfulness, their actions prove (at that time) they do not truly trust Him to solve the difficulty he or she is going through.

Jesus is teaching me how to have high expectation in Him; at this time Satan is forcefully attacking my mind. I refuse to be intimidated, moved by fear, or confused by the unwanted thoughts that are attempting to develop into unproductive emotions. My choice is to glorify God. I am going to stand firm, and live in His triumph because I walk by faith and not by sight. *"While we look not at the things which are seen, but at the things which are not seen: for the things which are seen are temporal: but the things which are not seen are eternal"* (*2 Corinthians 4:18*).

The devil is the father of all lies; he wants each person to be deceived by his misleading words. Satan should never be trusted, it is impossible for him to tell the truth. Until Jesus comes back in the sky to rapture His church, every child of God will be in a continuous warfare with him! Always remember Jesus has given us victory over the evil one!

In this was manifested the love of God toward us, because that God sent his only begotten Son into the world, that we might live through him. Herein is love, not that we loved God, but that he loved us, and sent his Son to be the propitiation for our sins.

1 John 4:9-10

Revelation

*I beseech you therefore, brethren, by the mercies of God,
that ye present your bodies a living sacrifice, holy,
acceptable unto God, which is your reasonable service.
And be not conformed to this world: but be ye transformed
by the renewing of you mind, that ye may prove what is
that good, and acceptable, and perfect will of God*

Romans 12:1-2

All honor and credit is to God, through His mighty influence the world was framed. Glory, majesty, dominion, and power both now and throughout eternity, (time without ending) belong to Him.

God wants each individual to give Him their bodies, thoughts, time, money, and every difficulty that will ever come into our lives. We must learn how submit everything to Him. Though, executing those actions in the right manner will take a process of time. Lord wants us to live in a manner which is according to His mighty power, righteousness, and excellent greatness.

Jesus requires each Christian to live holy and righteous lives. It's impossible for people who have a desire to fulfill the lustful longing that are within the flesh, to be pleasing to God. When individuals submit themselves to Him, their actions will become compliant to His Word. The immoral demands of the flesh are corrupt, and want only to fulfill sinful exploits, nothing good dwells within it. Its desires are in total disagreement to everything, which concerns God's righteousness demands. His Spirit wars against the issues that are inside of the flesh. The flesh is hostile and against His righteousness demand.

"Now the work of the flesh are manifest, which are these, Adultery, fornication, uncleanness, lasciviousness, idolatry, witchcraft, hatred, variance, emulations, wrath, strife, seditions, heresies, envyings, murders, drunkenness, revellings, and such like: of the which I tell you before, as I have told you in time past, that they which do such things shall not inherit the kingdom of God" (Galatians 5:19-21).

Before the human race was created a spiritual warfare between God and Satan took place. Iniquity was found in Lucifer (Satan), he deceitfully influenced a third of God's angels to turn against Him. This war continued when the serpent (the devil) tricked Eve. God told Adam not to eat from the tree of the knowledge of good and of evil. It was his responsibility to inform his wife. Eve believed the fruit was good for food, pleasant to the eyes, and it would make her like God. Those three fleshly thoughts lead Eve to be disobedient. She ate a piece of the fruit, and gave some to Adam. When he ate his portion, sin immediately came into the world.

Jesus also had to fight this warfare; He experienced this spiritual struggle after He had fasted for forty days and forty nights. The Lord was tempted by the devil three times to do actions that were not in God's will. In the Garden of Gethsemane Jesus had another spiritual confrontation; His human side did not want to undergo the adversities that He knew was getting ready to transpire.

This warfare was so intense, the Word utters, *"And being in agony he prayed more earnestly: and his sweat was as it were great drops of blood falling down to the ground" (Luke 22:44).* Jesus said, *"Father, if thou be willing, remove this cup from me; nevertheless not my will, but thine, be done" (Luke 22:42).* The Lord suffering in this way demonstrated to us the procedure, which must be used, when going through difficult circumstances. We must allow the will of God to rule in our life, He wants every believer to always receive the triumphant.

The body of Christ will continue fighting this spiritual war until Jesus raptures His church. The battle against sin won't end until Satan, his angles, and every person that would not accept Jesus as their Lord and Saviour are put in the lake of fire for eternality. It is written. *"And the devil that deceived them was cast into the lake of fire and brimstone, where the beast and the false prophet are, and shall be tormented day and night for ever and ever" (Revelation 20:10). "And whosoever was not found written in the book of life was cast into the lake of fire" (Revelation 20:14-15).*

Choose Jesus today!

If a man therefore purge himself from these, he shall be a vessel unto honor, sanctified, and meet for the masters use, and prepared unto every good work.

2 Timothy 2:21

Revelation

I marvel that ye are so soon removed from him that called you into the grace of Christ unto another gospel. Which is not another: but there be some that trouble you, and would pervert the gospel of Christ.

Galatians 1:6-7

Total praise without ending belongs to God; He manifested Himself in the form of Jesus, and gave His life on each person's behalf. The Lord was predestined to experience the painful, humiliating, and undeserved affliction He received. He is the Lamb of God that was slain before the foundation of the earth.

God is eternal (has no beginning or ending). He created all things, and without Him nothing was made. *"For by him were all things created, that are in heaven, and that are in earth, visible and invisible, whether they be thrones, or dominions, or principalities, or powers: all things were created through him, and for him" (Colossians 1:16).* God gave the first man and woman authority over the earth. Nevertheless, they made an extremely unwise decision to be disobedient to His command. Adam's defiant deed had deadly consequences on the human race. As a result to his rebellious action an evil spiritual being received those rights, which made him (Satan) the god of this world.

It is written, *"And I will put enmity between thee and the woman, and between thy seed and her seed; it shall bruise thy head, and thou shalt bruise his heel" (Genesis 3:15).*

Through those Words God promised the coming of the Messiah, and Him receiving victory over the devil (and sin). *Galatians 4:4-5* fulfills *Genesis 3:15,* it states, *"But when the fullness of time was come, God sent forth his Son, made of a woman, made under the law. To redeem them that were under the law, that we might receive the adoption of sons."*

The prophet Isaiah boldly declared, *"He was oppressed, and he was afflicted, yet he opened not his mouth: he is brought as a lamb to the slaughter, and as a sheep before her shearers is dumb, so he openeth not his mouth. And he made his grave with the wicked, and with the rich in his death; because he had done no violence, neither was any deceit in his mouth" (Isaiah 53:7, 9). "He shall see of the travail of his soul, and shall be satisfied: by his knowledge shall my righteous servant justify many; for he shall bear their iniquities" (Isaiah 53:11).* The things that Isaiah prophesied about Jesus was said hundreds of years before His birth, nevertheless, the prophet's words came to pass.

Jesus was born; died, and resurrected by the mighty power of the Holy Ghost. The Scriptures boldly states, *"Knowing that Christ being raised form the dead dieth no more; death hath no more dominion over him. For in that he died, he died unto sin once; but in that he liveth, he liveth unto God" (Romans 6:9-10).* In another place it declares, *"Which he wrought in Christ, when he raised him from the dead, and set him at his own right hand in the heavenly places. Far above all principality, and power, and might, and dominion, and every name that is named, not only in this world, but also in that which is to come" (Ephesians 1:20-21).*

Through God's mighty power and His extraordinary intelligence, He made a way for Himself to receive a human body. God is Jesus revealed in the flesh. The Lord came to earth in the likeness of a man to redeem mankind; He is the Saviour of the world. *"And all things are of God, who hath reconciled us to himself by Jesus Christ, and hath given to us the ministry of reconciliation. To wit, that God was in Christ, reconciling the world to himself, not imputing there trespasses unto them; and hath committed unto us the word of reconciliation" (2 Corinthians 5:18-19).*

Please do not be deceived! The Word tells us, *"Beware of false prophets, which come to you in sheep's clothing, but inwardly they are ravening wolves" (Matthew 7:15). "Take heed that no man deceive you. For many shall come in my name, saying, I am Christ; and shall deceive many" (Mark 13:5-6). "Little children, it is the last time: and as ye have heard that an'-ti-christ shall come, even now are there many an'-ti-christs; whereby we know that it is the last time" (1 John 2:18).* Jesus does not want anyone to be confused or misled. The devil's greatest weapon is deception, be very cautious in regards to what you choose to believe.

"Who is a liar but he that denieth that Jesus is the Christ? He is an'-ti-christ, that denieth the Father and the Son" (1 John 2:22). The spirit of antichrist is functioning on the earth at this time; it controls people that are in total disagreement with Jesus Christ. They refuse to believe and won't accept Him as their Saviour. Satan is the antichrist (manifested in the flesh) he will one day be revealed. The devil wants to stop every individual he can from accepting Jesus, the Author of eternal life.

Surrender to Jesus today!

But though we, or an angel from heaven, preach any other gospel unto you than that which we have preached unto you, let him be accursed. As we said before, so say I now again, If any man preach any other gospel unto you than that ye have received, let him be accursed.

Galatians 1:8-9

Revelation

Behold, I shew you a mystery; We shall not all sleep, but we shall all be changed. In a moment, in the twinkling of an eye, at the last trump: for the trumpet shall sound, and the dead shall be raised incorruptible, and we shall be changed. For this corruptible must put on incorruption, and this mortal must put on immortality.

1 Corinthians 15:51-53

All praise and majesty belongs to Jesus Christ. This transformation (corruptible to incorruption and mortal to immortality), will one day come to past. Every knee shall bow and every tongue shall confess that Jesus is Lord to the glory of God.

Through God's unconditional love, abundant mercies, and amazing grace He made a way for each person's sins to be forgiven. Jesus is going to give each individual that believed and surrendered to Him eternal life. *"And this is the will of him that sent me, that every one which seeth the Son, and believeth on him, may have everlasting life: and I will raise him up at the last day" St. John 6:40.*

The coming of the Messiah will be an extraordinary and powerful event. Every person that wants to be a part of the rapture must be born again. *St. John 3:3, 5* clearly states, *"Verily, verily, I say unto thee, Except a man be born again, he cannot see the Kingdom of God." "Verily, verily, I say unto thee, Except a man be born of the water and of the Spirit, he cannot enter into the Kingdom of God."* Each individual needs to have a rebirth experience.

Jesus is coming back for a church that is prepared and waiting for His miraculous and glorious return. The amount of time in which it takes for a person to blink their eyes, is how long it will take for those extraordinary actions to be fulfilled. He tells us, *"Behold, I come quickly; and my reward is with me, to give every man according as his work shall be. I am Al'-pha and the O-me'-ga, the beginning and the end, the first and the last" (Revelation 22:12-14).* A saint's godly duty is to encourage as many people as they can to surrender to the Lord.

The last trumpet (of salvation) shall sound; however, everyone won't be able to hear it. Believers that are in their graves and the saints who died, and their bodies were destroyed, will receive spiritual bodies, through the overwhelming authority of God's power. *1 Corinthians 15:42-44* tells us, *"So also is the resurrection of the dead. It is sown in corruption; it is raised in incorruption. It is sown in dishonor; it is raised in glory: it is sown in weakness; it is raised in power. It is sown a natural body; it is raised a spiritual body. There is a natural body, and there is a spiritual body."* Those believers shall be caught up to meet Jesus in the sky. *"For the Lord himself shall descend from heaven with a shout, with the voice of the archangel, and with the trump of God: and the dead in Christ shall rise first" (1 Thessalonians 4:16).*

Individuals that did not accept Jesus as their Saviour, skeletons will remain in their graves until **"The Day of Judgment."** *Revelation 20:11* declares, *"And I saw a great white throne, and him that sat on it, from whose face the earth and the heaven fled away: and there was found no place for them. And I saw the dead, small and great, stand* *before God: and the books were opened: and another book was opened, which is the book of life: and the dead were judged out of those things which were written in the books according to their works" (Revelation 20:11-12).*

People will be asleep and others wide awake performing daily responsibilities at homes, on jobs, schools, and many other places. Some are going to be riding in vehicles, airplanes, and trains. On that day, what they are doing or their location will not be significant. The only thing that is going to make a difference at that time is them having a personal relationship with Jesus Christ. *"Then we which are alive and remain shall be caught up together with them in the clouds, to meet the Lord in the air" (Thessalonians 4:17).* Only those who are in the body of Christ will perceive the rapture is taking place

The Lord is going to elevate every born again believers' natural body. Their bodies will be similar to helium filled balloons, when they are rising up into the atmosphere. Close your eyes and envision yourself to be lifting up into the heavens. Most people have heard the old saying, "What goes up must come down." Since the earth was put upon its foundation, this (the massive power of gravities) has been true, however, it won't be so when those things are taking place. Millions perhaps billions of people are going to rise up into the sky to meet Jesus. He is going to overpower the force of gravity. When those astounding things are taking place, gravities' great authority won't have any influence over the believers' bodies.

The Lord will change (this is the last transformation) the believers vile bodies so they will be recreated, in the likeness of His glorious body. The saints will stand before **"The Judgment Seat of Christ."** *2 Corinthians 5:10,* clearly tells us, *"For we must all appear before the judgment set of*

Christ; that every one may receive the things done in his body, according to that he hath done, whether it be good or bad." Jesus has personally invited every person; we all have been given an invitation to His great marriage feast. **MAKE SURE YOUR RESERVATIONS ARE INSTANTLYE RECOGNIZED!** *"Blessed are they which are called unto the marriage supper of the Lamb" (Revelation 19:9).*

> *But of the times and the seasons, brethren, ye have no need that I write unto you. For yourselves know perfectly that the day of the Lord so cometh as a thief in the night.*
>
> *1 Thessalonians 5:1-2*

Likewise, ye wives, be in subjection to your own husbands; that, if any obey not the word, they also may without the word be won by the conversation of the wives. Likewise, ye husbands, dwell with them according to knowledge, giving honour unto the wife, as unto the weaker vessel, and as being heirs together of the grace of life; that your prayers be not hindered.

1 Peter 3:1,7

Chapter 7

Love and Submit

*Husbands, love you wives, even as Christ also
loved the church, and gave himself for it.*

Ephesians 5:25

Expressions of appreciation and praise belong to the Lord.

Jesus was made high priest forever, as an outcome of Him triumphantly accomplishing the actions He achieved at Calvary. **Hebrews 6:20** tells us, **"Whither the forerunner is for us entered, even Jesus, made an high priest for ever after the order of Mel-chis'-e-dec."** God gave each husband the same influence in their marriages that He granted to Jesus Christ in regards to His church.

Jesus wants every husband to have faith, study His Word, and pray. He will honor every sincere prayer that they request on their families behalf. Husbands have a responsibility to love, provide, and take care of the needs of their family unit. They set the atmosphere in their homes **(good or bad)**! Married men that are believers should trust Jesus (without doubting) to fill them with the Holy Ghost. As a result they will be given unlimited supernatural authority to take care of their families in the Spiritual realm, through the mighty influence of His power. The

Word declares, *"But ye shall receive power, after that the Holy Ghost is come upon you" (Acts 1:8).*

Most married men were not taught how to be good husbands. They saw their fathers' bad examples when he mistreated and disrespected their mothers. Some of them heard harsh words, and saw different forms of abuse taking place, which embedded bad perceptions in their minds. The lack of a fathers' presence made other serious issues that many husbands have to deal with. Despite those unproductive consequences, through God's compassion being revealed in His Word, they can learn how to effectively love their wives.

A husband has an important responsibility, to be a protective covering over his family. For an example when a cover is over a bed, the cover will symbolize the husband; it protects the sheets from every substance. The top sheet will be an illustration of his wife, with the flat sheet representing their children. If a liquid was poured on the bed it would have to go through the cover before it could touch either sheet. Likewise nothing should be able to hurt or overwhelm a man's wife or children (those that are under his control) before it goes through him. A husband's obligation is to protect them from every opposition. If the top or flat sheet were over the cover it would be incorrect. Wife never attempt to obtain authority in regards to your husband. Children should always be obedient to their parent's rules.

As a bad influence of some married men's anger, hidden insecurities, and selfish motives, they verbally and physically abuse the women they promised to love for better or worse. God is not pleased when those things are taking place. Each husband ought to truly judge themselves by the Lord's standards. Married men are usually wrong when problems are occurring in their marriages because they are not performing their responsibilities in the manner Jesus instructed!

Communication is extremely important; learn how to talk to your wife in the right way. Discuss complicated concerns with her using loving and kind words. Never say bitter, disrespectful, or hurting expressions to your wife that could make her feel brokenhearted and insecure. Do not make small difficulties into gigantic problems. The Word declares, *"So ought men to love their wives as their own bodies. He that loveth his wife loveth himself. For no man ever yet hated his own flesh; but nourisheth and cherisheth it, even as the Lord the church" (Ephesians 5:28-29).*

Married men have been given a great obligation to provide their families' needs. Those who are not implementing that duty correctly need to seek employment. Jesus is waiting to open doors of opportunity. The Word tells us, *"But my God shall supply all your need according to his riches in glory by Christ Jesus" (Philippians 4:19)*

When your wife wants to have sex with you do not deny her. The Word clearly states, *"Likewise the husband hath not power of his own body, but the wife" (1 Corinthians 7:4).* A husband has a fulfilling duty to satisfy their wife's sexual needs. Do not be a selfish lover, learn how to be passionate. Be willing to change some of your moves! There is an intimacy in sex that God wants each married couple **(that is between a man and woman)** to encounter.

Married men should have an overwhelming commitment which motivates them to perform each action they need to accomplish to make their wives live joyful, blessed, and extremely fulfilling lives. Each husband ought to encourage their wives to develop into the greatest individuals that they can become. Every married woman should feel loved, respected, and appreciated.

If you are being unfaithful to your wife, by committing the sin of adultery stop being a part of that unholy affair. Pray for deliverance, with Jesus' assistance she will be able to forgive you. **However, this is an extremely delicate issue that should be handled very cautiously.** Get control over your body, mind, and fleshly desires. Do not permit yourself to be sexually attracted or satisfied by another woman. **It is a sin before God.**

The Bible tells us, *"But I say unto you, That whosoever looketh on a woman to lust after her hath already committed adultery in his heart" (Matthew 5:28).* Husbands, these words signify that when a man look intently at a woman, longing to be with her sexually, adultery has been committed (in their hearts) because of those lustful desires. If married men could feel the sadness, brokenhearted emotions, and damaging thoughts that forcefully attack their wives mind (because they can perceive their husbands are being driven by a lustful spirit) they would not permit themselves to be constrained by those sinful longings. **Jesus has given each husband (that truly submits to Him) victory in every area of their lives. Trust Him to deliver you!**

Husbands, if you are having secret sexual imaginations about another woman stop. Do not permit yourself to be demonically restricted in that manner. This is a serious concern; always remember, God knows all things, He can discern the thoughts and intents of every person's mind and heart. Cast down those immoral imaginations in the name of Jesus. Do not be misled or controlled by lustful feelings. Meditate on the Word of God; every person will be accountable for their actions.

A person should be able to perceive a married man's character in his wife's face and demeanor. Can fear, uncertainty, physical or mental abuse be seen? Is low self-esteem, sadness, or any other unproductive emotion detected in her appearance? Would those feelings be a consequence to his unfaithfulness, heartless word, or the other insensitive actions that he performs?

Husbands cannot obtain (godly) victory if their wives feels unloved, disrespected, or abused (verbally, physically, mentally, or sexual). They can only receive unconditional success when love, respect, forgiveness, and the difficulties of life are shared between the two of them. Jesus wants each husband's leadership to govern every issue that concerns their marriage.

> *"For the man is not of the woman; but the woman of the man. Neither was the man created for the woman; but the woman for the man."*
>
> *(1 Corinthians 11:8-9)*

Love and Submit

*Husbands, love your wives, and
be not better against them.*

Colossians 3:19

Recognition will always belong to God. He manifested Himself in the flesh, as the man, Jesus Christ. Through His examples He gave each husband a perfect illustration to use when they are attempting to love their wives.

Husbands should love their wives, in the manner that Christ loved His Church (using an unconditional and unchanging compassion). They ought to devote quality time to the women they married. However, on many occasions, some husbands will unwisely show more attention and consideration to other people's needs. Those men should be very cautious because Satan is sending out many deceiving distractions, trying to lead them the wrong way. **Proverbs 14:12** tells us, *"There is a way which seemeth right unto a man, but the end thereof are the ways of death,"*

A husband must not allow feelings of intimidation to exist inside of his wife, pertaining to something she thinks he is going to say or do. She ought to feel secure relating to the confidence she can entrust in his love. A married man's wife's wellbeing should be his greatest concern. It ought to be impossible for another person to compare to her because of the manner that he has built her up, in his mind

The Lord is loving, merciful, and kind. He longs to forgive, direct, and extend grace. Jesus has never done any type of hurtful or negative action to a person that is in the Body of Christ. He promised to give them victory in every area of their lives. Each husband should use the examples He demonstrated. It is written, *"Husbands, love your wives, even as Christ also loved the church, and gave himself for it: That he might present it to himself a glorious church, not having spot, or wrinkle, or any such thing; but that it should be holy and without blemish" (Ephesians 5:25, 27).*

At times married men say extremely hurting words to their wives, thinking that those remarks are okay. The Word clearly states, *"But he that doeth wrong shall receive for the wrong which he hath done: and there is no respect of person" (Colossians 3:25).* Husbands need to learn how to discuss problems, without using harsh or unkind words. Don't break your companion's heart, by the way you choose to talk to her. God is going to hold every married man accountable, for the procedure in which they use to take care of His daughters.

Jesus chose every saved husband to be good examples to unsaved men and boys. They should perform this great responsibility and honor to the best of their ability, judging themselves so He will not have to judge them. It is written, *"For unto whomsoever much is given, of him shall be much required" (Luke 12:48).*

> *Let us therefore, as many as be perfect, be thus minded: and if in any thing ye be otherwise, minded, God shall reveal even this unto you. Nevertheless, whereto we have already attained, let us walk by the same rule, let us mind the same thing.*
>
> *Philippians 3:15-16*

Love and Submit

*Likewise, ye husbands, dwell with
them according to knowledge, giving honour
unto the wife, as unto the weaker vessel,
and as being heirs together of the grace
of life; that your prayers be not hindered.*

1 Peter 3:7

All praise, glory, and expressions of gratitude are deeply inside of my heart to God because He revealed Himself to me, through His beloved Son, Jesus the Anointed One.

The love that Jesus has for His Church is the strongest act of compassion that exists. Marriage is the next profound feelings of affection. He tells every husband to love their wives in the same method, which He demonstrated. ***"FOR THIS CAUSE SHALL A MAN LEAVE FATHER AND MOTHER AND SHALL CLEAVE TO HIS WIFE: AND THEY TWAIN SHALL BE ONE FLESH" (Matthew 19:5).*** The husband has a responsibility to make this wonderful relationship begin and to be remarkable in every manner.

The unlimited and perpetual love God has for the human race motivated Him to show them mercy. He used His extraordinary plan of salvation to reveal those massive feelings of affection. The Lord knew every individual's extreme need of a Redeemer. Through His actions He made a way for each person (who would believe) to escape standing before **"The Great White Throne of Judgment."** Jesus' exploits proved His massive feelings of love.

It is impossible for a married man that mistreats his wife to have a healthy relationship with God **(repent if you are guilty)**. He gave each husband authority to godly influence their marriages. Married men should love their wives in a way that gives the Lord glory! Husbands, do your jobs well before God.

> *But I would have you know, that the head of every man is Christ; and the head of the woman is the man; and the head of Christ is God.*
>
> *1 Corinthians 11:3*

Love and Submit

*Wait on the LORD: be of good
courage, and he shall strengthen
thine heart: wait, I say, on the LORD.*

Psalms 27:14

All authority and power belongs to Jesus now and forever.

One Sunday morning after the message was powerfully preached, I was baptized. A few months later, I received the Holy Ghost (with the utterances of speaking in another tongue). An overwhelming desire existed within me that longed to declare those things to Stan. My desire was to tell him about the important, however, not completely understood spiritual experiences that took place. When I came home from church on both of those days, the spirit of anger could be perceived in my husband's face. It was not a good time to tell him about the breathtaking actions which had occurred. He would have gotten angrier, and we did not need any added perplexities in our lives.

It looked like we began to speak different languages, with me choosing to verbalize words that were glorifying to God.

Stan and I appeared to be changing into a couple which came from different and unfamiliar places. The two of us had been in this very challenging relationship for many years. However, at this time we were becoming strangers to each other. Jesus changed me from being controlled by the influence of sin, to being justified through His mighty redeeming power. An irresistible desire to live immorally wrong, no longer constrained my life. Stan did not understand the transformation which took place. He perceived it was a part of me that he could not control.

When those things were occurring my husband was selfish and demanding. Nevertheless, I had a duty to please him. Performing loving and submissive actions demonstrated his happiness was my greatest concern. The Lord did not want me to give Stan a reason to become jealous or intimidated, by my new and very fulfilling relationship with Him. Not attempting to say I did everything right.

Over a period of time the Lord empowered me to fight a triumphant battle. My words might sound foolish but they are not. They have proven themselves to be true. God exploits irrational and unjustified situations to bless and develop His people. The most exceptional years that Stan and I were together followed our marriage and my salvation. At this time he does not have a problem with me being saved. One day my husband will permit his life to be ruled by Jesus' mighty power.

But they that wait upon the LORD
shall renew their strength; they
shall mount up with wings as eagles;
they shall run, and not be weary; and
they shall walk, and not faint.

Isaiah 40:31

Love and Submit

*And they that know thy name will put their
trust in thee: for thou, LORD, hast not forsaken
them that seek thee. Sing praises to the LORD, which
dwelleth in Zion: declare among the people his doings.*

Psalms 9:10-11

All admiration and glory belongs to Jesus; He is extremely impressive in all of His ways. It would be impossible for a person to explain or understand the extraordinary, supernatural, and mind-blowing actions He has triumphantly accomplished.

I've been saved for twelve years; nevertheless, my companion has not come to church with me. Only God can give Stan a genuine desire to truly surrender to Him. One day he is going to receive a greater longing to seek the Lord and be delivered from his sinful way of living. Many prayers and words of thanksgivings have been said on his behalf.

When Stan gets an opportunity to talk to my brothers and sisters who are in Christ, he will perceive God's love coming out of them. On one occasion my husband met Pastor Cannon, nevertheless, at that time he did not have a desire to come to church. As an effect of God's great love, He set Stan up at a mutual place, where my companion felt comfortable, and believed he had some control.

My pastor turned fifty, and his wife and sisters gave him a birthday celebration. The event was held at the place where Stan worked. My husband had to assist Mother Cannon, her sisters-in-law, and several other people on the evening before the festivity. The following night Stan, our children, and I went to the birthday celebration. However, while we were there he was working overseeing the building.

Do not think Pastor Cannon's birthday event being at the place where my husband worked was a coincidence. Stan got a chance to meet some of God's beloved children because of that celebration. He had a great time and warmly received each person. A love is now growing within his heart for them.

God will demonstrate wonderful acts of kindness on each person's behalf. He deeply loves the human race. It is written, *"The LORD has appeared of old unto me, saying, Yea, I have loved thee with an everlasting love: therefore with loving kindness have I drawn thee"* (Jeremiah 31:3).

Trust in the LORD with all thine heart;
and lean not unto thine own understanding.
In all thy ways acknowledge him, and
he shall direct thy path. Be not wise in thine
own eyes; fear the LORD, and depart from evil.

Proverb 3:5-7

Love and Submit

Wives, submit yourselves unto your own husbands, as it is fit in the Lord.

Colossians 3:18

All praise and recognition belongs to Jesus.

Stan and I had a great longing to live in sin, when our relationship began. The devil ruled our lives; we were consumed by the powers of darkness. The two of us had to endure many bad consequences because of the way we chose to live. There were various problems that could have been avoided. My husband was wrong most of the time, although Stan believed he was always right, and in the heat of a disagreement, he would not change his mind.

My husband periodically got stressed out about our deficient funds. Those issues created complications in our marriage. Stan would get angry with me because of the pressure he was under. I was not able to assist him with our financial difficulties, nevertheless, in the spiritual realm I sustained him in ways he could not comprehend. The blessings of God were spoken over his life in my prayers every day.

The Lord told me not to argue with my husband when difficult situations were taking place. When he was no longer upset, I would have a conversation with him concerning the problem or problems. Our misunderstandings were solved faster using that approach. My opinions could be explained more precisely, Stan listened, and was more considerate to the words I declared.

Jesus wanted me to submit to my husband in a greater manner. A desire began to develop within my heart to assist him in ways I refused to do in the beginning. Positive statements had to be declared to Stan, regardless of the difficulties that were taking place. I had to learn how to become a godly submissive wife.

Stan came home from work one day declaring, his employers did not pay him for the holiday. In addition he stated we were not going to be able to pay all of our bills. My husband gave me money for groceries and other necessities. While he was talking I believed every word that he said. Following those things being proclaimed, **"Mrs. Submissive"** replied, do not worry everything is going to work out. After we finished talking Stan decided to go outside.

My husband had a briefcase that was sitting on our dresser. Curiosity alone with an undeniable desire came within me to look in it. As an outcome to those feelings, I glanced inside of the briefcase. His check stub was in it, and to my shock, he had received a full check. It could clearly be seen without an uncertainty, my husband lied to me. His thoughtless and inconsiderate deeds were very disturbing.

I began to question Jesus, seconds later He profoundly stated, "Your husband is not going to reward you for submitting to him, I Am. I will also make Stan surrender to you." The Lord distinctly proclaiming those very insightful words helped me to forgive my husband. I did not say anything to him, in regards to the things that took place.

Jesus began to reveal other difficulties to me that Stan was going through. At first those concerns were very upsetting, because I was not handling them in the right way. My responsibility was to trust Him, to give us victory over those issues. The Lord did not want me to judge Stan's inadequacies. I'm learning how to victoriously accomplish that great deed of love.

Wives, ought to be forgiving, respectful, and encouraging to their husbands. I ask God to give married women a supernatural drive which compels them to be loving and submissive. Not declaring we should not address problems that are taking place. I am saying it needs to be done in a respectful way and at the right time. Do not permit yourselves to be influenced by the way complexities appears, sounds, or feels, we must live our lives through faith in Jesus Christ. He wants each married couple to receive victory in every situation.

For the husband is the head of the wife,
even as Christ is the head of the church:
and he is the saviour of the body.

Ephesians 5:23

Love and Submit

Therefore I say unto you, What things soever ye desire, when ye pray, believe that ye receive them, and ye shall have them.

Mark 11:24

God is all powerful, there is not anything too complicated for Him to accomplish.

One night I asked Stan to visit my church, on the following Sunday. My husband challenged me, by saying he was hungry. When his words were being said, I was lying on our bed relaxing not too many seconds from being sleep. However, to a great extent in Stan's mind, his wishes being fulfilled came before him coming to church, so I got up and made him a sandwich.

My husband was acting very grumpy, on the morning that he was invited to church. He asked, if he could stay at home and come the following Sunday. Stan's question revealed to me, I had the upper hand. Regardless to his bad attitude my reply remained the same. He got disturbed about several small concerns, before we got into our car, however, I could not let myself be troubled by those things.

Stan was coming to church with his family for the first time. Happiness as well as excitement overflowed within me, though those feeling could not be revealed. While we were going to True Worship Church my husband boldly declared, "I am leaving church as soon as service ends. If you are riding home with me, be ready to walk out the door."

When we entered the church, I could perceive, my husband felt comfortable, he happily greeted the saints. While Pastor Cannon was preaching, Stan could not take his eyes off of him; tears began to roll down his face. My companion tried very hard not to let me see him crying, he did not understand the things that were taking place.

Whitney, Stanley, and I quickly got up, and walked out of the sanctuary following the morning message. We remembered my husband's words relating to us leaving church, however, he was acting different. Stan walked toward us declaring that he wanted to talk to Pastor Cannon. With a warm smile, he quickly turned around, and went back into the sanctuary. My husband's attitude had changed, so I waited in the vestibule thanking and glorifying God.

Jesus blessed Stan in a wonderful way that morning. My responsibility is to wait patiently until his day of salvation comes. Having assurance in God's Word, His faithfulness, and patience, will help me to withstand, until my husband's transformation is completed.

*And above all these things put on charity,
which is the bond of perfectness. And let the
peace of God rule in your hearts, to the which also
ye are called in one body; and be ye thankful.*

Colossians 3:14-15

Love and Submit

*(**F**or we walk by faith, not by sight.)*

2 Corinthians 5:7

Nonstop praise and honor without conclusion belongs to Jesus Christ now and throughout eternity. He has continuously shown mankind His undeserved love, mercy, and amazing grace.

Each individual should be willing to suffer on Jesus' behalf, only the things that are done for Him will make a difference at the end! *"For this is thankworthy, if a man for conscience toward God endure grief, suffering wrongfully. For what glory is it, if, when ye be buffeted for your faults, ye shall take it patiently? But if, when ye do well, and suffer for it, ye take it patiently, this is acceptable with God. For even hereunto were ye called: because Christ also suffered for us, leaving us an example, that ye should follow his steps" (1 Peter 2:19-21).*

My sister-in-law was having problems in her marriage. God used me to encourage Faith when those things were taking place. One day finding the right words to say to her was extremely challenging. I wanted to utter phrases that would have given my sister-in-law hope

Faith needed to trust Jesus, regardless to how trying the circumstances appeared. When those issues were happening she did not stop loving and submitting to her husband. However, surrendering to him was difficult for Faith to do because of the various times he neglected his responsibilities regarding their marriage. Jimmy was acting very self centered.

The Lord wanted my sister-in-law to give those problems to Him. One day we decided to pray and fast about the things that were taking place. Her husband was performing irresponsible actions which had many unnecessary consequences. After those problems were given to Jesus, Jimmy began to act more loving, trustworthy, and respectful to his wife's needs and desires.

My sister-in-law was willing to experience unjustified unhappiness, loneliness, lack, and so many other things. God can use her actions, as an example of unquestionable love. Faith's acts of submission will help married women not to give up, but to endure until they receive victory in their marriages. Her devoted deeds demonstrated God's love in action.

Faith refused to divorce Jimmy; she could see greatness in him, at his lowest point. At this time they are seeking God together, trusting Him to work out their problems. People that know how to pray, please make appeals on their behalf. Prayers also need to be requested for every marriage to be blessed and strengthened by the power of God.

Jesus wants each wife to be instruments of righteousness. They should be loving, forgiving, and have positive attitudes. The Lord is going to reward every married woman that was obedient in this manner. A wife submitting to her husband is a form of worship to God. Through His mighty power and married women's acts of love (faith in His Word, prayer, and submission) their husbands will become the men He created them to be.

It is not spiritually, mentally or physically healthy for wives attention to be focused on disturbing actions which happened in the past or negative things they think might take place. If their husbands have not truly submitted to

Jesus Christ, they need to trust Him to totally deliver those men. Each wife ought to have high expectations in His faithfulness. The Word declares, *"Likewise, ye wives, be in subjection to your own husbands that, if any obey not the word, they also may without the word be won by the conversation of the wives" (1 Peter 3:1).*

Husbands that have surrendered to Jesus, and are born again, need their wives love, prayers, and faithfulness. The adversary is at all times attempting to overwhelm their minds with unproductive thoughts. Satan is sending out death defying assaults against those men, trying to overcome them with doubt, pride, and fear. He uses anger, unforgiveness, lust, and such like spirits, attempting to control their minds. The devil wants them to feel ineffective, confused, and hopeless. He longs to mentally paralyze and destroy every husband that believes and have confidence in Jesus Christ, the Saviour of the world.

For many years, I asked God to give Stan a greater desire to become the spiritual leader over our family, other prayers were requested. After sometime passed thanksgivings and praise began to come forth to Jesus, in regards to the wonderful actions I was anticipating Him to bring to pass. Though it looked like nothing had changed; God heard and fulfilled each appeal. The amount of time it took for those supplications to be seen in the natural realm was not important.

Many trying situations took place in our marriage; however, I could not dwell on those problems. Despite the countless times Stan allowed Satan to forcefully attack me, through his words and actions. My assurance had to rest in Jesus. He did not want me to meditate on the negative thoughts, which at times forcefully assailed my mind. Those deliberations had to be cast down and rejected.

One day Stan got into some trouble, the difficulties that occurred had nothing to do with his job. Nevertheless, his employers fired him because of issues which revolved around that situation. When those things were happening, my husband felt broken, overwhelmed, and hopeless. After Stan realized there was not a person who could beyond a doubt solve this problem, he began to submit himself to *El-Shaddai (The God who is all sufficient).*

Stan perceived Jesus longed to assist him to overcome this problem. My husband started to go to church with me. God began to convict him about sinful actions he enjoyed doing. The only way that conviction could have taken place in his heart is through the power of the Holy Ghost. He got baptized in the name Lord Jesus Christ.

Satan longed to completely devastate our family when those difficulties were taking place. His desire is to kill and eternally destroy every individual. He is totally evil; there is not anything righteous or good inside of him. However, the intense influence that came from the problems which took place, led Stan to seek Jesus. Through His awesome power He used each complexity, as if they were powerful magnets that drew my husband closer to Him. One day Stan will surrender to the Only Living God!

But ut thanks be to God, which
giveth us the victory through
our Lord Jesus Christ.

1 Corinthians 15:57

Love and Submit

*Likewise, ye wives, be in subjection
to your own husbands; that, if any obey
not the word, they also may without the
word be won by the conversation of the
wives. While they behold your chaste
conversation coupled with fear."*

I Peter 3:1-2

Perfect praise without conclusion belongs to Jesus. He performed the greatest act of love when He submitted His life, as a living sacrifice on each person's behalf.

Wives submitting to their husbands in this generation, appear to be extremely challenging for the majority of them to do. Although they should be accommodating in every way and offer consideration to their husband's needs. *Ephesians 5:22* tells us, *"Wives, submit yourselves unto your own husbands, as unto the Lord."* God made the husband head of the wife. *"For the husband is the head of the wife, even as Christ is the head of the church; and he is the saviour of the body" (Ephesians 5:23). "For the man is not of the woman: but the woman of the man. Neither was the man created for the woman: but the woman for the man" (1 Corinthians 11:8-9).*

Most girls did not see married women surrendering to their husbands, in the right way, while they were growing up. For many years my mother was a single parent; she was not able to teach me those things. I did not have a sound understanding, in regards to the manner a wife should act. Over a period of time God gave me correct instructions through His Word.

Many wives have been discouraged by unkind words and inconsiderate actions their husbands said or did. Those men's thoughtless deeds damaged the women's emotions that they had a great responsibility to love, protect, and cover. Their unwise reactions were controlled by hopeless feelings of anger, fear, and insecurity. Misleading spirits transported unhappiness, confusion, and such like attitudes, inside of them.

Married women should be a blessing to their companions even when issues appear to be totally extreme, unfair, and hard to understand.

Do not allow yourself to be overwhelmed at those times. Regardless to how difficult problems become, wives should not permit themselves to be influenced by unproductive thoughts or feelings. Stand on God's Word, Its forever true, and will withstand until the end of time. Rejoice in all things good and bad; refuse to be a disobedient wife!

"Who can find a virtuous woman? For her price is far above rubies. The heart of her husband doth safely trust in her, so that he shall have no need of spoil. She will do him good and not evil all the days of her life" (Proverbs 31:10-12). Jesus wants each wife to live honorable and righteous lives. He longs to develop a virtuous personality inside of each married woman.

The Lord is teaching me how to love Stan unconditionally. *1 Corinthians 13:4-7 tells us, "Charity suffereth long, and is kind; charity envieth not; charity vaunteth not itself, is not puffed up, doth not behave itself unseemly, seeketh not her own, is not easily provoked, thinketh no evil; Rejoiceth not in iniquity, but rejoiceth in the truth; beareth all things, believeth all things, hopeth all things and endureth all things."* His Word does not state that love triumph over some things it profoundly declares, **"ALL THINGS!"** My prayer is for the Lord to permit *1 Corinthians 13:4-7* to be extremely effective inside of each married woman's heart.

Wives don't be consumed by trying issues, unproductive thoughts, or hard to comprehend situations your husbands created. Trust God to workout those difficulties. Never allow your emotions to develop into unhappiness, lack of confidence, or apprehension. Don't permit yourself to come to the ultimate decision, "I cannot take this any longer, I want a divorce! God is not glorified by those words.

Each wife needs to convey an unconditional and unchanging love to their husbands, regardless to the situations that are taking place. Married women should always make uncompromised choices to forgive them. Forgiveness is an extremely important factor in each marriage. *"For if ye forgive men their trespasses, your heavenly Father will also forgive you. But if ye forgive not men their trespasses, neither will your Father forgive your trespasses" (Matthews 6:14-15).*

Married women that think their lives are in danger; should find a place of safety, as soon as possible! There are organizations, family members, and churches that will assist women to overcome this type of difficulty. Be prayerful and seek a place of refuge!

Husbands have a need within themselves to know the actions God created them to achieve. However, they might not reveal that necessity to their wives, because of concealed uncertainties, confusion, and pride. Married women should ask the Lord to reveal to their companions the exploits; He chose them to accomplish. There are times that some married men (unwisely) won't receive their wives' insightful opinions. Do not become unhappy at those periods, Jesus has given your marriages the victory, have confidence in Him and that triumph will come to pass.

It is not mentally healthy for married women to be consumed by unproductive and brokenhearted feelings, in regards to issues, which happened in their marriage. Neither should they allow their thoughts to focus on hopeless sentiments that came from previous relationships. The devil wants to deceive each wife to be broken in spirit, hopeless, and to the point of hating someone in the chambers of their mind.

A wife ought to be compassionate to her husband. She should long to satisfy his sexual desires. The Word clearly states, *"The wife hath not power of her own body, but the husband" (1 Corinthians 7:4).* Sex between a married couple (man and woman) is a breathtaking, exhilarating, and extremely satisfying experience that was ordained by God.

If a married woman refuses to fulfill her husband's sexual needs, the devil longs to anoint another young lady that won't reject his desires.

Be very careful! Do not send your husband into the arms of another woman. Pray, if there is a problem in that area, Jesus can renew your sexual relationship, making it more satisfying at the end, than what it was in the beginning.

A person should be able to perceive a married woman's character in the face and demeanor of her husband. Does his appearance illustrate confusion, low self-esteem, or unhappiness? Would it be a consequence to his wife's selfish actions, disobedient attitude, unfaithfulness, or unkind words?

If you're being unfaithful to your husband (by committing the sin of adultery) God is not pleased, get control over your body and mind. **This is an extremely delicate matter, which should be handled very cautiously.** *Matthew 5:28* tells us, *"But I say unto you, That whosoever looketh on a woman to lust after her hath committed adultery with her already in his heart."* This scripture also means, when a woman looks at a man yearning to be with him, adultery has been committed in her heart. If you are having secret sexual thoughts about another man stop. Do not allow your mind to be imprisoned by those sinful deliberations. Pray for deliverance (if any of these things are taking place). The Lord is going to hold every married woman accountable for their actions.

Wives must become skillful in regards to the weapons they were given to put into operation, before, and when difficulties are taking place. Love, prayer, and patience are conquering artilleries that must be utilized to powerfully influence objectionable circumstances. Ask the Lord for instructions and the ability to do the actions that need to be accomplished. Don't waste time being doubtful or apprehensive. Trust in the exploits Jesus faithfully performed, He made a way for each husband and each wife to receive uncompromised victory in their marriage.

Trust in the LORD, and do good; so shalt thou dwell in the land, and verily thou shalt be fed. Delight they self also in the LORD; and he shall give thee the desires of thine heart. Commit thy way unto the LORD trust also in him; and he shall bring it to pass.

(Psalm 37:3-5)

And nd he is before all things and by him all things consist. And he is the head of the body, the church: who is the beginning, the first born from the dead; that in all things he might have the preeminence. For it pleased the Father that in him should all fullness dwell. And, having made peace through the blood of his cross, by him to reconcile all things unto himself; by him I say, whether they be things in earth, or things in heaven.

Colossians 1:17-20

Chapter 6

From the Pastor's desk

But the hour cometh, and now is, when the true worshippers shall worship the Father in spirit and truth: for the Father seeketh such to worship him. God is a Spirit: and they that worship him must worship him in spirit and in truth.

St. John 4:23-24

True Worship Church is a purpose driven church, which was specifically created to meet people's needs. We are seeking the excellence of God. Jesus designed our godly organization to serve, love, and direct a countless number of individuals out of sin to the Only Living God. This mission will be accomplished through our presence in the community. We desire to help them with their spiritual and natural needs. Our objective is to encourage each person to set goals and achieve them. ***Philippians 1:6*** tells us, ***"Being confident of this very thing, that he which hath begun a good work in you will perform it until the day of Jesus Christ."*** We will share our faith and teach people that through trusting in God, and having confidence in themselves there are no limits to what they can accomplish.

I (Pastor Lovell Cannon Jr.) intend to make myself available to people in the same manner that many individuals made themselves accessible to my needs. They told me about the gospel of Jesus Christ. After being obedient to the gospel's demands, He changed the sinful actions in which I at one time longed to perform. God delivered me from drugs, alcohol, and gambling, He stopped me from running the streets to running a race for Him. At this time I am a Holy Ghost filled preacher who ministers the gospel of Jesus Christ. He added to my life a very loving and supportive wife, Tina, as well as four wonderful children Sherri, Lovell III, Tiffany, and Jathan.

I accepted my calling to the ministry in 1982 while attending a bible institution, attempting to study to show myself approved unto God. Love, respect, and a great concern for people are my greatest aptitudes and strengths. I desire to give one hundred and fifty percent of myself. The ability to counsel and identify with young gang members and drug users is based on twenty years of practical street knowledge and public relation skills.

Youth in the city of Detroit need spiritual leaderships and this is something I desire to do. God gave me a vision to open a church. I am extremely dedicated and patient in regards to the different visions which He chose me to accomplish. Through His faithfulness and mighty power, some of those things have already come to pass and the others will one day be fulfilled.

As a direct result of the triumph Jesus received on the Cross, our faith in the things He accomplished, personal experiences, and the power of the Holy Ghost, True Worship Church is a haven of hope to many souls. Jesus directs people who are lost in sin, unhappy, fearful, and confused to our church so they can receive complete deliverance. Our desire is to help children, teenagers, adults, and families to have great potential in their lives. We will demonstrate love and illustrate consideration for other's needs. This great purpose will be achieved through hard work and devotion. Accomplishments attained during our many years of ministry will be assets readily drawn upon as we endeavor to:

* Establish group meetings for the homeless.
* Conduct marriage counseling seminars.
* Continue Evangelistic Outreach for the Youth.
* Maintain Prison Outreach Ministries.
* Assist various youth programs:
    1. P.A.L.
    2. Young men and women for Christ.
* Mentor the young people within the community.
* Evangelize the neighborhood.

"One thing have I desired of the LORD, that will I seek after; that I may dwell in the house of the LORD all the days of my life, to behold the beauty of the LORD, and to enquire in his temple." (Psalm 27:4) "I had fainted, unless I had believed to see the goodness of the LORD in the land of the living; Wait on the LORD: be of good courage, and he shall strengthen thine heart: wait, I say, on the LORD" (Psalm 27:13-14).

I (First Lady Tina Cannon) would like to thank my Saviour, Lord Jesus Christ for giving me a desire to live a life of holiness. Though there will be many tests and trials. The believer's life is full of joy, faith, hope, and love. In all things a person will receive total victory if they keep their eyes on Christ. This is my testimony! God filled me with the Holy Ghost at the age of nine. I loved going to church and being around the people of God.

A lot of my training came from the many years in which I was listening, watching, and sitting under His Word. As a result to me receiving the Holy Ghost at a very young age, many challenges came into my life. I unwisely chose to hang out and experience some of the negative things that the world had to offer, however, not fitting in.

While walking to church my prayers would be for the Lord to give me a greater desire to live for Him. Over a period of time, He faithfully answered those request. Through His grace I had a chance to turn around and totally surrender to Him. Jesus is so good, trustworthy, and full of compassion. He loved me when I did not love myself; He is a deliverer, keeper, friend, and way maker!

Every individual must learn how to WAIT on the LORD. When they wait on Him they will always be TRIUMPHANT! At the times we assume things are over and it would be impossible for us to receive the victory, He comes through on our behalf! While an individual is waiting, Jesus longs to give them instructions to the things they need to do or stop doing so they will receive a boundless triumph in each difficulty.

Jesus wants to teach us how to cry and get results. When a person cries out and calls on His name, He hears them. Do not think for one minute that He does not perceive the sound of an individual's cry; we must learn how to totally trust in Him! *"And it shall come to pass, that before they call, I will answer; and while they are yet speaking, I will hear" (Isaiah 65:24).* Always remember, **PEOPLE THAT PRAY AND WAIT ON GOD ARE WINNERS!**

We (Pastor Lovell and First Lady Tina Cannon) have been given an undisputable desire to tell people about the gospel of our Lord and Saviour Jesus Christ. Our desire is to effectively proclaim Jesus' life, death, and resurrection. He wants every person to know, *"All things are of God, who hath reconciled us to himself by Jesus Christ, and hath given to us the ministry of reconciliation. To wit, that God was in Christ, reconciling the world unto himself, not imputing their trespasses unto them; and hath committed unto us the word of reconciliation. Now then we are ambassadors for Christ, as though God did beseech you by us: we pray you in Christ's stead, be ye reconciled to God"* *(2 Corinthians 5:18-20).*

FROM THE PASTOR'S DESK

7 Reasons for the Baptism in the name
"Lord Jesus Christ"

1. IT IS APOSTOLIC IN ORGIN AND PRACTICE. *(Acts 2:38, 4:12, Col 3:17)*

2. We are exhorted to believe and obey the teachings of the apostles.

3. The three commissions do not contradict each other. *(Matthew 28:19, Luke 24: 45-48, Mark 16:15-16)*

4. To put on Christ we must be baptized into His death and burial. *(Romans 6:4)*

5. We are saved by believing in the name of Jesus. *(Proverbs. 18:10, Acts 4:12, 1 John 2:12)*

6. Father, Son, and Holy Ghost are not proper names, but titles expressing the great three fold manifestation of:

   (1) God-the Father in creation
   (2) Son-in redemption
   (3) Holy Spirit-in the regeneration in the church

   The command in *Matthew 28:19* is to baptize in the name LORD JESUS CHRIST.

7. JESUS IS ALL IN ALL *(Matt. 1:21-23, John 1:1-4, 1:14, Col 2:9-10, Col 3:11, 1 Timothy 3:16, 1 John 5:20)*

From the Pastor's Desk
MINISTRY OF THE HOLY SPIRIT

CONVICTS THE SINNER

John 16:8-13 "...he will reprove the world of sin and of righteousness and of judgment."

Conviction is the first step in a sinner being saved. The Holy Spirit anoints the Word that is being preached. He quickens it in the heart and conscience of a person awakening them to an awareness of their lost condition and causes him or her to see themself a sinner. An individual could never repent from their sins until they first experience a Holy Ghost conviction. Salvation is the work of the Holy Spirit in a person's heart from beginning to end.

REGENERATES

John 3:5 "Except a man be born of water and of the Spirit he cannot enter into the kingdom of God."

Titus 3:5 "...by the washing of regeneration and renewing of the Holy Ghost.

The work of regeneration is changing a sinner into a saint, causing an individual to become a new creation in Christ Jesus. After a person believes the finished works that Jesus accomplished on the Cross, and receive Him as their Lord and Saviour their regeneration begins. Following those actions taking place, the believer should trust Him (beyond a shadow of a doubt) to fill them with His Spirit.

DWELLS INSIDE OF THE CHILD OF GOD

Roman 8:9 "…if so be that the Spirit of God dwell in you."

1 Corinthians 6:19 "…your body is the temple of the Holy Ghost which is in you."

The Holy Spirit fills the temple and abides there.

SEALS

Ephesians 1:13 "In whom also after that ye believed, ye were sealed with the Holy Spirit of promise."

To be sealed means the following.

(I)   Ownership: The children of God now belong to Jesus Christ.

(II) Security: The children of God are safe as long as the seal is never broken.

(III) Approval: The seal places God's approval on each believer.

(IV) Finished Work: The baptism of the Holy Ghost is the last act in the work of regeneration in the life of the believer. However, the work of growth and sanctification continues.

AFTER A PERSON IS FILLED WITH GOD'S SPIRIT THEY WILL RECEIVE UNLIMITED POWER

Acts 1:8 "But ye shall receive power, after that the Holy Ghost is come upon you."

The word "power" comes from the same root as the word "dynamite." This is the power of God coming into the life of an individual, which gives them power to live victoriously over sin. It additionally gives authority to each Holy Ghost filled person to witness the awesome saving grace of Jesus Christ to the unsaved.

INTO THE BODY OF CHRIST

1 Corinthians 12-13 "By one Spirit are we all baptized into one body."

The believer is placed into the body of Christ, and in a process of time, the Spirit of God comes inside of them. This may be illustrated by placing an empty cup into a pail of water. The cup is in the water and the water is in the cup.

GUIDES THE CHILD OF GOD

The Holy Spirit gives God's children an understanding of the Scriptures and His will. He wants to guide us in every detail of our lives; each person has a responsibility to seek the sound of His voice and to study the Scriptures.

References: John 16:13 Romans 8:14
Act 13:2-4 Act 16:6-7

*A*nd Jesus came and spake unto
them, saying, All power is given
unto me in heaven and in earth.

Matthew 28:18

Chapter 8

The power of God

*That I many know him, and the power of his
resurrection, and the fellowship of his suffering,
being made conformable unto his death. If by any means
I might attain unto the resurrection of the dead.*

Philippians 3:10-11

Continuous praise, glory, and worship without ending
belong to God.

Through God's vast love He created mankind to have
a personal and very intimate relationship with Him.
The King of all kings desires to have an extremely close
connection with every individual that should never be
broken. However, Adam broke that connection, as an
outcome of his sin. Sin disconnected mankind from
a loving and faithful God. *"For as in Adam all died"*
(Corinthians 15:22).

Jesus wants to reveal the directions to eternal salvation
to each individual. Every person has been given a great
accountability to truly ask Him questions about His great
deliverance plan. Liberation starts in an individual's heart
that will make a strong conviction come inside of their

mind. After a human being feels it, they should surrender to the Only Living God.

As a powerful effect of the authoritative action Jesus performed (His blood coming out of His body) He made a way for our iniquities to be forgiven. *"For without the shedding of blood there is no remission" (Hebrews).* A person surrendering to the Lord is the greatest choice they could ever decide. An individual is required to repent, and believe, He gave His life on their behalf. They must truly accept Him as his or her Lord and Saviour. Jesus longs to fill every believer with the Holy Ghost, so they will have power to live in a manner that is accounting to His perfect will and fight a good fight of faith.

The Lord gave each person an opportunity to take part in this union. He won't force anyone to love Him. Individuals, that choose to be rebellious, refusing to submit to the Lord, will receive the final consequences of their wrong decisions. The scripture clearly states, *"But the fearful, and unbelieving, and the abominable and murderers, and whoremongers, and sorcerers, and idolaters, and all liars, shall have their part in the lake which burneth with fire and brimstone which is the second death" (Revelation 21:8).* This penalty is too high of a price for anyone to be willing to pay. **Be wise make Jesus your Saviour today!**

Jesus wants us to create a consecrated and holy atmosphere. He should be glorified regardless of the place, time, or situations that are taking place. The Lord longs for the Body of Christ to bombard the heavens with praise and worship. He is coming back (in the sky) to receive every person who received Him as their Lord and Saviour. After that amazing event take place, we will praise and worship the God of eternal life throughout perpetuity.

O GOD, thou art my God; early will I seek thee:
my soul thristeth for thee, my flesh longeth for
thee in a dry and thirsty land, where no water is.
To see thy power and thy glory, so as I have seen thee
in the sanctuary. Because thy lovingkindness
is better than life, my lips shall praise thee.

Psalm 63:1-3

The power of God

*But seek ye first the Kingdom of God,
and his righteousness; and all these
things shall be added unto you.*

Matthew 6:33

God wants each person to be a partaker of His **"Heavenly Divine Kingdom."** Praise and appreciation belong to Him.

Something extremely powerful and very exhilarating began to take place. Jesus transformed my sinful nature to a righteous character. He gave me authority over the power of sin! Through the Lord's mighty supremacy, I was changed from being a servant of the devil to a child of the Only Living God. I started to seek things that were pertaining to His righteousness.

Months later I perceived that God wanted to bless His children spiritually and naturally. He had consecrated me in the most imperative manner. I no longer had to stand before Him in judgment. In place of a perpetual sentence, the Lord made it possible for me to be with him forever and receive rewards. *"Henceforth there is laid up for me a crown of righteousness, which the Lord, the righteous judge, shall give me at that day and not to me only, but unto all them also that love his appearing" (2 Timothy 4:8).*

Months later I unwisely began to pursue material possessions. My attention started to focus on getting a job, a great amount of time was wasted thinking about or looking for employment. I went to a community center which was seeking people to work for them. An individual within that establishment declared they were going to hire me for a soon coming assignment. However, when it was time for the job to start they hired someone else. Confusion and unhappiness profoundly grew within my mind because I truly believed Jesus was going to give me that job.

Over a period of time I realized it was impossible for me to seek God in the right way if my thoughts were being preoccupied by worldly desires. Working could have terminated the assignments He chose me to successfully accomplish. Jesus can distinguish the assets in which He can allow His beloved to receive. It is written, *"Lay not up for yourselves treasures upon earth, where moth and rust doth corrupt, and where thieves break through and steal. But lay up for yourselves treasures in heaven, where neither moth nor rust doth corrupt, and where thieves do not break through nor steal" (Matthew 6:19-20).*

The Lord won't give people possessions which are in disagreement to His Word. Each individual should be very careful in regards to the things they ask Him to do. *"For where your treasure is, there will your heart be also" (Matthew 6:21).* God's delight is to give His beloved children wonderful spiritual and natural benefits. *"Eye hath not seen, nor ear heard, neither have it entered into the heart of man, the things which God prepared for them that love him" (1 Corinthians 2:9).* Jesus has a great desire to grant us outstanding and unbelievable resources, His answers are always yea and amen to the request that agrees with His Word.

One thing have I desired of the LORD, that will I seek after; that I may dwell in the house of the LORD all the days of my life, to behold the beauty of the LORD, and to enquire in His Temple.

Psalm 27:4

The power of God

He that loveth father or mother more than me is not worthy of me: and he that loveth his son or daughter more than me is not worthy of me.

Matthew 10:37

Unlimited praise and majesty belongs to Jesus now and until the conclusion of time. He has an eternal Kingdom that will never end.

The Lord began to give me insight to extraordinary biblical truths that was not always understood. Extremely confusing scriptures now made sense. I attempted to tell my mother several of those spiritual topics. At times she got angry because she could not comprehend those revelations.

My mother tried to live a good life. Nevertheless, her respectable character was not enough. She needed to submit to God by believing in Jesus Christ. My mother did not commit great sins. Yet, she was born with a sinful nature that had to be changed. The Lord longed to deliver her from living immorally wrong. The Word states, *"Come unto me, all ye that labour and are heavy laden, and I will give you rest. Take my yoke upon you, and learn of me; for I am meek and lowly in heart: and ye shall find rest unto you souls. For my yoke is easy, and my burden is light"* *(Matthew 11:28-30)*

Jesus began to reveal Himself to my mother; she was now ready to talk to me about His great salvation plan. Over a period of time my mother received Jesus as her Lord and Saviour. Before she died He filled her with the Holy Ghost. My mother will have fellowship with Him throughout infinity. All glory and majesty without ending belongs to the Only Living God!

Every believer must witness the gospel to their families, friends, and each person that will listen. Jesus wants the saints to go to different areas in their city, state, country, and other parts of the earth. The Word declares, *"Go ye into all the world, and preach the gospel to every creature" (Mark 16:15).* Through the saint's righteous examples, people will be able to perceive they can live holy and honorable lives.

> *The harvest truly is plenteous, but the laborers are few. Pray ye therefore the Lord of the harvest, that he will send forth laborers into his harvest."*
>
> *Matthew 9:37*

The power of God

*Lo, children are an heritage of the LORD: and the
fruit of the womb is his reward. As arrows are in
the hand of a mighty man; so are children of the youth."*

Psalm 127:3-4

Thanksgivings, honor, and praise will always belong to
Jesus now, and throughout eternity. He manifested Himself
in the resemblance of sinful flesh. Jesus is our Lord and
Redeemer; He is the Lion of the tribe of Judah.

Following the morning message being preached, my
youngest son agreed to tarry (wait) for the Holy Ghost.
In the beginning, Stanley did not want to do this action;
he was being accommodating to my wishes. When those
things were happening, I had an unfruitful thought that
Stanley might not receive God's Spirit because of the way
he was acting. My way of thinking made me the hindering
factor!

Jesus wanted Stanley to have a greater longing to receive
His Spirit. I encouraged my son to praise God in the
beginning. Another missionary started to godly influence
him; he needed to yield himself to Jesus Christ. Stanley
began to sincerely praise the Lord, after he truly submitted
to Jesus; He filled him with His Spirit.

On that day God fulfilled one of the promises He
guaranteed me relating to my children. His Word
proclaims, *"For the promise is unto you, and to your
children, and to all that are afar off, even as many as the
Lord our God shall call" (Act 2:39).* In another place it is

written, *"The Lord is not slack concerning his promise, as some men count slackness; but is longsuffering to us-ward, not willing that any should perish, but that all should come to repentance" (2 Peter 3:9).*

My husband called me on the telephone, while we were talking he quietly listened to every word that I said, in regards to our youngest son being filled with the Holy Ghost. The two of us were filled with excitement and wonder. After he came home Stanley was the first person he wanted to talk to.

Stan questioned Stanley concerning the things that happened while we were at church. He asked him, "How did it feel when you received the Holy Ghost? What did it feel like when you began to speak in another tongue?" God filling Stanley with the Holy Ghost gave his father a greater desire to know more about a person receiving His Spirit.

Jesus' ultimate desire is to save every person. It is not a complexity too hard for Him to solve, nor is there a man, woman, or child too difficult for Him to deliver from their sins. As soon as a person feels His Spirit convicting them, they should submit to the Lord while there is an opportunity. He wants each individual to know, **"Today is the day for salvation"** because tomorrow is not promised to anyone.

Train up a child in the way he should go: and when he is old, he will not depart from it.

Proverbs 22: 6

The power of God

I will bless the LORD at all times:
his praise shall continually be in
my mouth. My soul shall make
her boast in the LORD: the humble
shall hear thereof, and be glad.
O magnify the LORD with me,
and let us exalt His name together.

Psalm 34:1-3

Constant praise without conclusion belongs to Jesus Christ. He is the Author of eternal life, the Commander of the angelic host.

I began to have a great desire to answer my telephone saying, "Praise the Lord." At first this action was very difficult to do. Saying hello for so many years when answering the telephone made changing those words challenging. However, my desire was to declare words that glorified Jesus. The Scriptures tells us, *"Blessed be the name of the LORD from this time forth and for evermore. From the rising of the sun unto the going down of the same the LORD'S name is to be praised"* (Psalm 113:2-3).

One night while being at church, Jesus blessed me, in a manner He had never done before. I began to answer the telephone saying, "Praise the Lord" after that astonishing supernatural experience happened, my longing was to live in a method, which honored God. Words were now being uttered by me that exalted Him. *Ephesians 4:29* tells us, *"Let no corrupt communication proceed out of your mouth, but that which is good to the use of edifying, that it may minister grace unto the hearers."*

When I answered my telephone saying "Praise the Lord" some of the people who called became offended. Nevertheless, I could not stop giving Jesus recognition because of how an individual felt or reacted. God had shown me so many wonderful acts of love and kindness. He should be acknowledged in every way. Yes! *"I will bless the Lord at all times and His praise shall continuously be in my mouth."* Everlasting admiration that has no conclusion belongs to Him. The Redeemer of mankind deserves boundless and nonstop praise. Amen and Amen!

> *To appoint unto them that mourn in Zion, to give unto them beauty for ashes, the oil of joy for mourning, the garment of praise for the spirit of heaviness; that they might be called trees of righteousness, the planting of the LORD, that he might be glorified.*
>
> *Isaiah 61:3*

The power of God

*Blessed be the God and Father of our Lord Jesus
Christ, who hath blessed us with all spiritual blessings
in heavenly places in Christ. According as he hath chosen
us in him before the foundation of the world, that we
should be holy and without blame before him in love.*

Ephesians 1:3-4

All credit, praise, and honor belong to Jesus; He is the Only
Living God.

My desire is to be committed to the preparations, and
concerns that are pertaining to the Lord, however, I have
foolishly rotated Him around many unwise decisions.
Satan attacked and mentally paralyzed my mind with
unproductive thoughts on various occasions. When those
difficulties were taking place, Jesus had already given me
the victory (at Calvary) though at that time I could not see
or feel that triumph **Romans 8:37-39** powerfully states,
**"Nay, in all these things we are more than conquerors
through him that loved us. For I am persuaded, that
neither death nor life, nor angels, nor principalities, nor
power, nor things present, nor things to come, nor height,
nor depth, nor any other creature, shall be able to separate
us from the love of God, which is in Christ Jesus our Lord."**

Through God's grace I am learning how to be obedient to
Him, even when conditions are hurtful, unfair, and hard
to understand. A great yearning is growing within me to
perform deeds that agree to His righteousness. He has
given me a great peace. The Scriptures declares, **"Thou
wilt keep him in perfect peace, whose mind is stayed on**

thee: because he trusteth in thee. Trust ye in the LORD for ever: for in the LORD JE-HO'-VAH is everlasting strength" *(Isaiah 26:3-4).*

Jesus wants us to stay in harmony with Him through, faith, studying His Word, and prayer. They are powerful spiritual tools that can be used to transport the victory that He made available to each believer into the natural realm. The Lord has chosen a peculiar people to be true worshipers; their desire is to live holy and sanctified lives. They do not worship God because of the things He can do for them, the saint's worship God because of who He is. *"But the hour cometh, and now is, when the true worshippers shall worship the Father in spirit and in truth: for the Father seeketh such to worship him. God is a Spirit: and they that worship him must worship him in spirit and in truth"* *(John 4:23-24).*

> Commit thy way unto the LORD; trust also in him; and he shall bring it to pass.
>
> *Psalm 37:5*

The power of God

*In his day Judah shall be saved, and
Israel shall dwell safely: and this
is his name whereby he shall be called,
THE LORD OUR ROUGHTEOUSNESS.*

Jeremiah 23:6

Jesus Christ is the Redeemer of the world. He should receive all praise.

This section contains some of the Names, Titles, and Characteristics of our Lord and Saviour Jesus Christ.

The Redeemer *And the Redeemer shall come to Zion, and unto them that turn from transgression in Jacob, saith the Lord. (Isaiah 59:20)*

The Chosen of God *And the people stood beholding. And the rulers also with them derided him, saying, He saved others; let him save himself, if he be Christ, the chosen of God. (Luke 23:35)*

God's First Born Son *And she brought forth her firstborn son, and wrapped him in swaddling clothes, and laid him in a manger; because there was no room for them in the inn. (Luke 2:7)*

The Seen of David *The book of the generation of Jesus Christ, the seed of David, the son of Abraham. (Matthew 1:1)*

The Seed of Women *And I will put enmity between thee and the woman, and between thy seed and her seed; it shall bruise thy head, and thou shall bruise his heel. (Genesis 3:15)*

The Son of Man *Saying, Behold, we go up to Jerusalem; and the Son of man shall be delivered unto the chief priests, and unto the scribes; and they shall condemn him to death, and shall deliver him to the Gentiles.: (Mark 10:33)*

The Son of the Living God *And Simon Peter answered and said, Thou art the Christ, the Son of the living God. (Matthew 16:16)*

The Only Begotten Son *No man hath seen God at any time; the only begotten Son, which is in the bosom of the Father, he hath declared him. (John 1:18)*

The Son of the Most High God *And cried with a loud voice, and side, What have I to do with thee, Jesus, thou Son of the Most High God? I adjure thee by God that thou torment me not. (Mark 5:7)*

Rabbi, Thou Art the Son of God *Nathaniel answered and saith unto him, Rabbi, thou art the Son of God; thou art the King of Israel. (John 1:49)*

The Christ, the Son of God *But these are written, that ye might believe that Jesus is the Christ, the Son of God; and that believing ye might have life through his name. (John 20:31)*

Jesus Christ is the Son of God *And Philip said, If thou believest with all thine heart, thou mayest. And he answered and said, I believe that Jesus Christ is the Son of God. (Acts 8:37)*

The Word *In the beginning was the word, and the word was with God and the word was God. (John 1:1)*

God Manifest in the Flesh *And without controversy great is the mystery of godliness; God was manifest in the flesh, justified in the Spirit, seen of angels, preached unto the Gentiles, Believed on in the world, received up into glory. (1 Timothy 3:16)*

The Highest *And thou, child, shalt be called the prophet of the Highest: for thou shalt go before the face of the Lord to prepare his way. (Luke 1:76)*

Saviour *And my spirit hath rejoiced in God my Saviour. (Luke 1:47)*

I am *Jesus said unto them, Verily, verily, I say unto you, Before Abraham was, I am. (John 8:58)*

The Lord *And it shall come to pass, that whosoever shall call on the name of the LORD shall be delivered: for in mount Zion and in Jerusalem shall be deliverance, as the LORD hath said, and in the remnant whom the LORD shall call. (Joel 2:32)*

The Alpha and the Omega *I am Alpha and Omega, the beginning and the ending saith the Lord, which is, and which was, and which is to come, the Almighty. (Revelation 1:8)*

I am the Resurrection and the Life *Jesus said unto her, I am the resurrection, and the life: he that believeth in me, though he were dead, yet shall he live. (John 11:25)*

The First and the Last *And when I saw him, I fell at his feet as dead. And he laid his right hand upon me, saying unto me, Fear not; I am the first and the last. (Revelation 1:17)*

The Brightness of His Glory *Who being the brightness of his glory, and the express image of his person, and upholding all things by the word of his power, when he had by himself purged our sins, sat down on the right hand of the Majesty on high; (Hebrews 1:3)*

The Image of God *In whom the god of this world hath blinded the minds of them which believe not, lest the light of the glorious gospel of Christ, who is the image of God should shine unto them. (2 Corinthians 4:4)*

Eternal Life *And we know that the Son of God is come, and hath given us an understanding, that we may know him that is true, and we are in him that is true, even in his Son Jesus Christ. This is the true God, and eternal life. (1 John 5:20)*

The Second Man, the Lord from Heaven *The first man is of the earth, earthy: the second man is the Lord from heaven. (1 Corinthians 15:47)*

The Seed of David *Concerning his Son Jesus Christ our Lord, which was made of the seed of David according to the flesh. (Romans 1:3)*

The Saviour of the World *And we have seen and do testify that the Father sent the Son to be the Saviour of the world. (1 John 4:14)*

The Head of the Body, the Church *And he is the head of the body, the church: who is the beginning, the firstborn from the dead; that in all things he might have the preeminence. (Colossians 1:18)*

The Head of All Principality and Powers *And ye are complete in him, which is the head of all principality and power. (Colossians 2:10)*

Emmanuel, God with Us *Behold, a virgin shall be with child, and shall bring forth a son, and they shall call his name Emmanuel, Which being interpreted is, God with us. (Matthew 1:23)*

Jesus Christ the Righteous *My little children, these things write I unto you, that ye sin not, and if any man sin, we have an advocate with the Father, Jesus Christ the righteous. (1 John 2:1)*

The Blessed *His name shall endure forever: his name shall be continued as long as the sun: and men shall be blessed in him: all nations shall call him blessed. (Psalm 72:17)*

The Deliverer *And so all Israel shall be saved: as it is Written, There shall come out of Si'-on the Deliverer, and shall turn away ungodliness from Jacob. (Romans 11:26)*

The Messiah the Prince *Know therefore and understand, that from the going forth of the commandment to restore and to build Jerusalem unto the Messiah the Prince shall be seven weeks, and threescore and two weeks; the street shall be built again, and the wall, even in troublous times. (Daniel 9:25)*

A Saviour *Of this man's seed hath God according to his promise raised unto Israel a Saviour, Jesus. (Acts 13:23)*

The Lord of Glory *Which none of the princes of this world knew: for had they known it, they would not have crucified the Lord of glory. (1 Corinthians 2:8)*

Lord Both of the Dead and Living *For to this end Christ both died, and rose, and revived, that he might be Lord both of the dead and living. (Romans 14:9)*

The Just One *Which of the prophets have not your fathers persecuted? And they have slain them which shewed before of the coming of the Just One; of whom ye have been now the betrayers and murderers. (Acts 7:52)*

The Prince of Peace *For unto us a child is born, unto us a son is given: and the government shall be upon his shoulder: and his name shall be called Wonderful, Counsellor, The mighty God, The everlasting Father, The Prince of Peace. (Isaiah 9:6)*

King of Kings, Lord of Lords *And he hath on his vesture and on his thigh a name written, KING OF KINGS, AND LORD OF LORDS. (Revelation 19:16)*

> *To whom also Abraham gave a tenth*
> *part of all; first being by interpretation*
> *King of righteousness; and after that also*
> *King of Salem, which is, King of peace.*
>
> *Hebrews 7:2*

The power of God

*And if children, then heirs; heirs of God,
and joint-heirs with Christ; if so be that we suffer
with him, that we may be also glorified together.
For I reckon that the sufferings of this present
time are not worthy to be compared with
the glory which shall be revealed in us.*

Roman 8:17-18

Bountiful praise without ending belongs to Jesus Christ; He humbled Himself, and became obedient unto death.

In the beginning of my salvation, I did not want to experience any type of unhappiness. It was very hard for me to understand how I could be blessed through suffering. However, the Word tells us, *"For our light affliction, which is but for a moment, worketh for us a far more exceeding and eternal weight of glory" (2 Corinthians 4:17). "And we know that all things work together for good to them that love God, to them who are the called according to his purpose" (Romans 8:29).*

People came against me many times. After those things happened my unwise reactions were to defend myself. God does not want an individual to use the wrong response when they are being challenged. I had to learn how to give answers that glorified Him in every confrontation. Hostile and insensitive words could not be said. I needed to develop a Christ like temperament. *"For what glory is it, if, when ye be buffeted for your faults, ye shall take it patiently? But if, when ye do well, and suffer for it, ye take it patiently, this is acceptable with God" (1 Peter 2:20).*

After dealing with problems on my own for too long, I gave them to Jesus. Through His Word He declared in *Ephesians 6:14-18*, *"Stand therefore, having your loins girt about with truth, and having on the breastplate of righteousness; And your feet shod with the preparation of the gospel of peace; Above all, taking the shield of faith, wherewith ye shall be able to quench all the fiery darts of the wicked. And take the helmet of salvation, and the sword of the Spirit, which is the word of God."*

I finally realized the devil was my enemy; he deceitfully used the people that can against me. However, they made the chose to be obedient to his deception. Through those circumstances I have developed into a stronger and wiser person. I no longer permit my thoughts to be focused on people or challenging situations.

The Lord gave us a protective covering to defend every part of our bodies except one (He does not cover a person's backs). Therefore we should never turn our backs to Satan. We must attack him using full force, exercising every weapon that has been granted to us, in the name of Jesus. For each saint to obtain victory they must have faith in the triumph Jesus received at Calvary. Prayer, fasting, and studying the Scripture are prevailing and extremely powerful artilleries that ought to be use daily. Believers should diligently seek the Lord to fill them with His Spirit; as a result they will obtain supernatural powers.

Praise and worship are spiritual devices which draw His Spirit into the atmosphere. The saints should never run from the devil; he should at all times be fleeing from them. Each born again believer must learn how to fight a good fight of faith, using its great authority to the fullest degree.

When a soldier goes on the battlefield they must have on all of their equipment. A qualified and successful fighter would never go on the front line of the combat zone with only parts of their battle gear. A defending force doing that would put his or her life in great jeopardy and others. It is an advantage when the armed forces know the plans and weapons of their opponents. A trained and obedient person, who has the ability to obey orders and to carry out commands, would make the best soldier.

We are in a spiritual battle twenty four hour a day, seven days out of each week, and three hundred and sixty five days out of every year that we live. The battle is for our souls. Through the love of God, Jesus has given us the triumph. At the end of this spiritual battle every person, who truly accepted Him as their personal Saviour will receive a crown of life.

> *But and if you suffer for righteousness' sake, happy are ye: AND BE NOT AFRAID OF THEIR TERROR, NEITHER BE TROUBLED.*

> *1 Peter 3:14*

The power of God

> *But God, who is rich in mercy, for his*
> *great love wherewith he loved us. Even*
> *when we were dead in sin, hath quickened us*
> *together with Christ, (by grace are ye saved;).*
> *And hath raised us up together, and made us sit*
> *together in heavenly places in Christ Jesus.*

Ephesians 2:4-5

Praise and eternal glory belong to Jesus Christ. He made a way for each person to visit Him in heavenly places. God's abundant mercy, grace, and quickening power belong to every individual that will receive it.

At one time great yearnings existed within me that wanted my fleshly desires to be satisfied. The penalties, which followed those actions, were not a concern. My longing was to live immorally wrong; I wanted to be where Satan's powers controlled the atmosphere.

God began to reveal to me, the consequences of my sinful lifestyle. Following that revelation, I realized a great price had to be paid for the way I chose to live. **"For the wages of sin is death!"** As a result to His abundant love and amazing grace, He made a way for me to escape that punishment. The Scriptures declared, **"But God commendeth his love toward us, in that, while we were yet sinners, Christ died for us" Romans 5:8.** Jesus paid the penalty for sin.

I submitted to Jesus, turned from sin to God. My spirit was revived and restored in His righteous. **"For Christ is the end of the law for righteousness to every one that** *believeth" (Romans 10:4). "Not by works of righteousness which we have done, but according to his mercy he saved us, by the washing of regeneration and renewing of the Holy Ghost; Which he shed on us abundantly through Jesus Christ our Saviour" (Titus 3:5-6).*

We are saved by the unmerited favor of God. People cannot do anything on their own accord that would make them deserve salvation. It is God's gift to mankind. The saving and delivering power of His Spirit convicts the heart of each unsaved individual. The conviction reveals their sinful condition.

As a prevailing effect to Jesus' life giving power, sinners are changed from being offenders of God, into righteous beings. He made it possible for them (those that believe in His salvation plan and accept Him as their Saviour) not to have a dreadful destination to receive the second death and eternal separation from God. The Word tells us, *"To the praise of the glory of his grace, wherein he hath made us accepted in the beloved. In whom we have redemption through his blood, the forgiveness of sin, according to the riches of his graces" (Ephesians 1:6-7).* Jesus gave each believer a glorious predestination to obtain eternal life, through them believing in Him, and the exploits He victoriously achieved.

Giving thanks unto the Father, which hath made us meet to be partakers of the inheritance of the saints in light. Who hath delivered us from the power of darkness, and hath translated us into the kingdom of his dear Son. In whom we have redemption through his blood, even the forgiveness of sins.

Colossians 1:12-14

The Spirit of the Lord is upon me,
because he hath anointed me to preach
the gospel to the poor: he hath sent me to heal
the brokenhearted, to preach deliverance to the captives,
and recovering of sight to the blind,
to set at liberty them that are bruised.
To preach the acceptable year of the Lord.

St. Luke 4:18-19

Chapter 9

Jesus is a healer, protector, and provider

*Trust in the LORD with all thine
heart; and lean not unto thine own
understanding. In all thy ways acknowledge
him, and he shall direct thy paths.*

Proverbs 3:5

All praise and appreciation belong to the Lord. He is a Powerful Protector.

One Sunday morning Whitney, Stanley, and I went to church. The three of us walked into the sanctuary and sat down. Not to many minutes later, Whitney looked at me with concern in her eyes, she asked, "Did you take your medicine?" A few seconds Stanley uttered the same remarks. After thinking about their question, my response was, no.

Whitney appeared to be comfortable; she did not say another word relating to that situation. However, Stanley gave the impression of being very nervous. My daughter and son had seen me have many seizures; their uneasiness could without difficulty be understood. Whitney and Stanley felt very uncomfortable if they thought it was a possibility for that illness to take place.

I told Stanley, he had to trust God to protect me. After those words were said, my son nervously sat back. Following him settling down, I began to pray these words; I plead the blood of Jesus against every demonic force that is attempting to attack me. The authority which is in Your blood is more powerful than any type of medicine, sickness, or evil power. Following those declarations being said these words began to come from within, *"Trust in the Lord with all of your heart and lean not unto your own understanding."* My reply was, Lord I trust You.

One of my duties (as being a missionary) was to help direct people to our pastor, so they could receive prayer, following the morning message. However, for a while I did not move; not too many minutes later, one of the mothers of our church signaled for me to come to assist them. I then went to the front of the sanctuary. After being there for a few minutes, I felt someone lightly kicking my leg. To my surprise Stanley had followed me to the front of the church.

When service was over my son stated, "Mama I trust God." All of the apprehension, which attempted to overwhelm him left. It might have been at least two hours before I could take my medicine, yet he no longer felt uneasy. Jesus awesomely demonstrated His defensive power to me on that day.

No weapon that is formed against thee
shall prosper; and every tongue that shall
rise against thee in judgment thou shalt condemn.
This is the heritage of the servants of the Lord,
and their righteousness is of me, saith the Lord

Isaiah 54:17

Jesus is a healer, protector, and provider

*Trust in the LORD, and do good; so
shalt thou dwell in the land, and verily thou
shalt be fed. Delight thyself also in the LORD; and
he shall give thee the desires of thine heart.*

Psalm 37:3-4

All praise and all glory belong to Jehovah Jireh, the God who promised to provide.

The Lord led me to Solomon's Temple; it was about thirty minutes from my house. I did not drive because of medical problems; therefore it was impossible for me to get to church on my own. However, issues that do not have a solution with a person's abilities are always possible through God's awesome power. He made a way for my children and me to be there every Sunday.

God's Word was truly being preached and taught at Solomon's Temple. The Scriptures are powerful; they can transform an individual's life. Jesus wanted me to be rooted and grounded in regards to things pertaining to Him. As a conclusion to those actions being done correctly the various visions He wanted me to accomplish would come to past.

Minister Clinton Cooper drove one of the church vans; he gave my children and me a ride to Solomon's Temple many times. Many individuals were taken to church, and some received salvation because of his faithful actions. Minister Clinton permitted the Lord to use him to do something that could've appeared to be insignificant; however, his obedient exploits were very pleasing to God. Great is his reward.

There were many Sundays that I didn't have any money to pay the people who gave me a ride to church; those individuals will receive compensation for their good deeds. Always remember you cannot do anything for Jesus or His beloved saints and not be rewarded! The Lord is so faithful, He promised to provide all of our needs; *"This I recall to my mind therefore have I hope. It is of the LORD'S mercies that we are not consumed, because his compassion fail not. They are new every morning: great is thy faithfulness"* *(Lamentations 3:21-23).*

> *It is a good thing to give thanks unto the LORD, and to sing praises unto thy name, O most High: To shew forth thy lovingkindness in the morning, and they faithfulness every night.*
>
> *Psalm 92:1-2*

Jesus is a healer, protector, and provider

But my God shall supply all your need
according to his riches in glory by Christ Jesus.

Philippians 4:19

All spiritually blessings come from our Lord and Saviour Jesus Christ, He is a Mighty Deliverer.

God has a vast love for the human race. He saw each individual in their sinful condition and had an enormous amount of sympathy. Through Jesus' triumphant exploits, He made a way for mankind to receive freedom over sin and death, canceling sin's deadly penalty. The Word tells us, *"O death, where is thy sting? O grave, where is thy victory? The sting of death is sin: and the strength of sin is the law. But thanks be to God, which giveth us the victory through our Lord Jesus Christ" (1 Corinthians 15:55-57).*

After Jesus revealed the exploits that He wanted me to accomplish, I did not want to work for another person. However, there were extremely trying times in which my husband needed help paying our bills. The different companies were threatening to turn our services off. We also received eviction notices, which made our family move at times that we were not prepared to relocate. When those things were happening it looked like I needed to be employed. Praise and glory belongs to God because He is a way Maker! He made a way for our bills to be paid, and He fulfilled every need. **Jesus will make a way when circumstances appear to be impossible.**

One summer my husband and I needed money to go on our family reunion. There were not any resources to pay for this trip, or to buy the necessities we wanted. A group of people owed the two of us a large sum of money. I gave that issue to Jesus in prayer. We received a letter not too many days later, stating those individuals owed us more than the amount calculated. My husband and I received that check the following week. Our family had more than enough money to do everything we wanted to do.

> *Now unto him that is able to do exceeding abundantly above all that we ask or think, according to the power that worketh in us.*

> *Ephesians 3:20*

Jesus is a healer, protector, and provider

*How God anointed Jesus of
Nazareth with the Holy Ghost
and with power: who went
about doing good, and healing
all that were oppressed of the
devil; for God was with him."*

Acts 10:38

Praise and glory belong to our Lord and Saviour Jesus Christ. He longs to empower each person with His Spirit, so they will be able to do great things. **Are you anointed by the mighty power of the Holy Ghost?**

One Sunday afternoon Bishop Bonner told our congregation to pray for four hours the next day and to fast. He declared we would be blessed because of our obedience. On that day I decided to pray over an unopened bottle of olive oil. Normally my pastor, an elder, or a minister at our church, would be asked to pray over the oil.

I realized God gave every person that was filled with His Spirit supernatural authority. Various problems were written on a piece of paper, I wanted the Lord to grant those supplications. An impact needed to be put inside of the oil that would bring deliverance to each person who was being oppressed by the powers of darkness.

The bottle of olive oil was in my hands for four hours, after praying I anointed myself. At that moment God's mighty influence came over me. All praise and all glory belongs to

Him because He anointed the oil. My thoughts were, "how much power did He put inside of it?"

Days later I decided to visit my mother, she was not feeling well. This dear woman had to take a test the next day at the hospital. She could not eat any food for twenty four hours; my mother also had to take some type of medicine that made her feel worst. After hearing those things I prayed, and anointed her with the oil. She then decided to lie down. My stepfather declared he was not feeling his best, and he asked me to pray for him.

I went to visit one of my mother's neighbors; she was a dear friend of our family for many years. On that day Sylvia had a headache; I prayed and anointed her with the oil. A few minutes later someone brought Sylvia some pain pill. She told them that she felt much better, and did not need to take any medicine.

When I went back to my mother's house she and my stepfather stated, the Lord healed them. What a mighty God! Jesus is all powerful and extraordinary in all of His ways! Within the same hour He healed my mother, stepfather, and their neighbor. What a mighty God!

> *Confess your faults one to*
> *another, and pray one four*
> *another, that ye may be healed.*
> *The effectual fervent prayers*
> *of a righteous man availeth much.*
>
> **James 5:16**

Jesus is a healer, protector, and provider

*Trust in the LORD, and do good; so shall
thou dwell in the land, and verily thou shalt
be fed. Delight thyself also in the LORD;
and he shall give thee the desires of thy heart.
Commit thy way unto the LORD; trust also
in him; and he shall bring it to pass.*

Psalm 37:3-6

All exaltation belongs to our Lord and Saviour. He is an uncontainable fire that has given every person who believes (in Him and the triumphs in which He accomplished) victory over the sin nature.

There were times God could not use me, my mind was focused on receiving various things His Word promised. Many personal possessions had not been received, so I unwisely attempted to get those objects on my own. Doing that made an opening for me to be distracted.

God appeared to be blessing other people, however, my family and I had not acquired the material belongings we needed and desired. It was hard for us to make ends meet. I needed to learn how to trust Him, despite the difficulties that were taking place. Regardless to how complicated the conditions became, Jesus wanted me to know, He is faithful and He would fulfill His promises.

My mind needed to be centered on God's Word, and I had to believe whatever it declared. Doing that taught me how to rejoice in each situation. *Ephesians 3:20* insightfully proclaim, *"Now unto him that is able to do exceeding abundantly above all that we ask or think, according to the power that worketh in us." 1 Corinthians 2:9* profoundly states, *"EYE HATH NOT SEEN, NOR EAR HEARD, NEITHER HAVE ENTERED INTO THE HEART OF MAN, THE THINGS WHICH GOD HATH PREPARED FOR THEN THAT LOVE HIM"*

When the devil sends out demonic assaults against God's people, he is not aware of how those attacks influence them, until their reactions. We should confuse him by the way we respond! Despite the tests and trails that are going to take place the saints must learn how to express joy. Jesus has given us victory in every situation at Calvary. He exploits extremely complicated issues to develop us, He want us to have faith that our triumph will come into the nature realm.

At this era of my life I'm fully persuaded, God is more than able to do everything that He has declared. Nothing is too hard for Him to accomplish. The Lord tells us in His Word, *"For I reckon that the sufferings of this present time are not worthy to be compared with the glory which shall be revealed in us." (Romans 8:18)* In another place it proclaims, *"But rejoice, inasmuch as ye are partakers of Christ's suffering; that, when his glory shall be revealed, ye may be glad also with exceeding joy. If ye be reproached for the name of Christ, happy are ye; for the spirit of glory and of God resteth upon you: on their part he is evil spoken of, but on your part he is glorified." (1 Peter 4:13-14)*

God does not want His people to be driven by the wrong desires; those longings could hinder or even stop individuals from fulfilling actions they were called to successfully accomplish. He wants every person to allow Him to put the right desires and correct thoughts within their mind. The Word states, *"Let nothing be done through strife or vainglory; but in lowliness of mind let each esteem other better than themselves. Look not every man on his own things, but every man also on the things of others. Let this mind be in you which was also in Christ Jesus"* *(Philippians 2:3-5).*

Jesus has unrestricted feelings of affection for mankind that is beyond their perception. His Word informs us, *"Greater love hath no man than this, that a man lay down his life for his friends" (St. John 15:13).* Each person needs to ask Him to forgiven them. They must believe, *"God so loved the world, that He gave His only begotten Son, that whosoever believe in him should not perish, but have everlasting life" (St. John 3:16).*

> *Though he slay me, yet will I trust in him:*
> *but I will maintain mine own ways before him.*

> *Job 13: 15*

Jesus is a healer, protector, and provider

But he was wounded for our
transgressions, he was bruised
for our iniquities: the chastisement
of our peace was upon him;
and with his stripes we are healed.

Isaiah 53:5

Jesus is the Great Healer; He is worthy to receive all praise and glory.

I started to have problems with my eyes; one of them began to cross. When that was happening, people looked at me in a different way. Individuals wouldn't look directly at my face they stared at the eye which began to cross.

Stan saw the difficulty which was occurring; however, he did not say a word relating to the problem. If my husband had made a negative comment in regards to this displeasing and unwanted condition, it would have been disturbing. Our oldest son (Jason) said something to me about that complexity. I felt very uncomfortable when his words were being spoken. Nevertheless, he confirmed my thoughts. The same issue happened to my mother's eyes. For me to be having that problem was truly unbelievable, this disorder had to be confronted and resolved.

I thought very deeply about the situation which was becoming visible. Deliberations went through my mind relating to things that could be done to correct this problem. I believed an eye doctor might be able to help me.

However, we did not have any medical insurance, or extra money. It was impossible for me to go to an eye doctor.

I had to give that problem to Jesus; He led me to apply His Blood to my eyes. Over a period of time many parts of the eye was learned and commanded to be one hundred percent whole in the name of Jesus because by His stripes I am healed. All thanks, credit, and eternal praise belongs to Him. In a process of time, through His awesome and very effective healing power, my eyes became one hundred percent normal. All glory belongs to God.

Who his own self bare our sins in his own body on the tree, that we, being dead to sin, should live unto righteousness: by whose stripes ye were healed.

1 Peter 2:24

Jesus is a healer, protector, and provider

He giveth power to the faint; and to them that have no might He increaseth strength. Even the youth shall faint and be weary, and the young men shall utterly fall. But they that wait upon the LORD shall renew their strength; they shall mount up with wings as eagles; they shall run, and not be weary; and they shall walk, and not faint.

Isaiah 40:29-31

Jesus Christ deserves eternal praise, glory, and majesty.

Jesus has granted His undeserved favor to each individual that is in the body of Christ, though at times they might become faint. The Word tells us, *"My grace is sufficient for thee: for my strength is made perfect in weakness" (2 Corinthian 12:9).* The Lord saw great potential inside of every person that would submit to Him. *"According as he hath chosen us in him before the foundation of the world, that we should be holy and without blame before him in love. Having predestinated us unto the adoption of children by Jesus Christ to himself, according to the good pleasure of his will" (Ephesians 1:4-5).* Through the power of His Spirit and His Word, He wants to teach us how to live righteousness, holiness, and triumphant lives.

Through the perfect and eternal atonement that Jesus accomplished at Calvary, He made a way for each sinner to receive deliverance. After He did those things, Jesus became our Great High Priest. *"Seeing then that we have a great high priest, that is passed, into the heavens, Jesus the Son of God, let us hold fast our profession. For we have not an high priest which cannot be touched with the feeling of our infirmities; but was in all points tempted like as we are, yet without sin. Let us therefore come boldly unto the throne of grace, that we may obtain mercy, and find grace to help in time of need" (Hebrews 4:14-16).*

Believers should long to be in God's presence. There are so many reasons why each person ought to rejoice in the Lord. He has an unconditional and unchanging love for every person. Jesus is the Only Living God, fulfillment and righteousness is totally in Him. He is the Author of eternal salvation, the Saviour of the world. Happiness, hope, and every other perfect and good gift are resting in the Messiah.

> *Wait on the LORD: be of good courage, and he shall strengthen thine heart: wait, I say, on the LORD.*
>
> *Psalm 27:14*

*Thou art worthy, O Lord, to receive
Glory and honour and power; for thou
hast created all things, and for thy
pleasure they are and were created.*

Revelation 4:11

Chapter 10

Honor

*Honour thy father and thy mother:
that thy days may be long upon the land
which the LORD thy God giveth thee.*

Exodus 20:12

Praise and honor belong to God.

There is a great desire within me to write this section in the memory of my dear mother, Lillian Burt Montgomery. She was not able to share or rejoice, in regards to the amazing and hard to believe exploits God chose me to accomplish. My mother tried very hard to teach her children the things we needed to know to obtain happy and successful lives. She was a faithful, loving, and kindhearted, person.

One of her responsibilities was to be a single parent. She had to do obligations that a father should have done. My mother taught us not to give up, regardless, to how complex the problems became. She did not compare or choose one child over the other, she loved us all. This dear woman knew how to show affection to her children in the manner in which each child needed. An endless love will always reside within my heart for her.

Using my mother's principles helped me to receive victory in many areas. Instead of complaining when we were having challenging times, words of assurance were said to Stan and our children. I would not condemn them concerning the difficulties we at times had to experience because of their unwise decisions. My choice was to speak words that helped them to develop into the greatest individuals they could become. Nor did I ever compare our conditions to a person who had achieved more worldly possessions.

My mother was an extremely independent individual. This dear woman had many outstanding qualities; she did not miss going to work, which made it possible for our bills to be paid. My mother had a great concern for the welfare of her children. On the other hand her autonomous spirit was not good because she began to depend on her abilities to fulfill our family's needs. Those things stopped my mother from having high expectations in God's faithfulness. As a result of His unrestricted love, great mercy, and amazing grace, He wanted to teach her how to have confidence in Him.

To our disappointment, my mother got sick; after she went to the doctor we were told she had colon cancer. However, it was removed; in addition my mother had to take chemotherapy treatments. Everything appeared to be going in the right direction. Her body was healing and she went back to work in a short amount of time.

The cancer returned about two years later, it had spread to three parts of her body. My mother became very weak. Nevertheless, I had to believe in God's healing power, regardless of how bad the situation appeared. I could not permit myself to become overwhelmed or doubtful because of the doctor's diagnosis.

My mother started taking radiation treatment with great hopes of it destroying the cancer. After her first treatment, we walked into the elevator, seconds later another young lady entered it. Both of us could perceive that she was not feeling her best. My mother asked, "How are you doing?" The young lady declared, "Not well."

While the young lady and my mother were talking I wanted to stop their conversation. I thought she might have said unkind words to my mother. Nevertheless, they continued to talk. She said a few more words of encouragement. Following her expressions the young lady's countenance brightened up, as if she received strength from the words that were declared. In my mother's very weak condition God found a way to use her to be a blessing to someone else.

Not long after my mother got sick, she died. Jesus exploited cancer, and used that illness as a powerful instrument with great expectations of drawing her closer to Him. As a result to those things happening, she began to have confidence in His faithfulness. Some of her last words were, "Vickie I want to be obedient to God." In the last and exceptionally difficult days of my mother's life He taught her how to trust Him.

It was very difficult to understanding why Jesus permitted my mother to die. I truly believed He would heal her. The Lord revealed to me that she successfully completed the most imperative test every person had to take. It is written, ***"I am the resurrection, and the life he that believeth in me, though he were dead, yet shall he live. And whosoever liveth and believeth in me shall never die. Believest thou this" St John 11:25-26?***

I believe with all my heart that one day I will see my mother in heaven.

Every person needs to make a decision to yield their lives to Jesus. Through the power of His Spirit, He will help them to live in a righteous manner. God longs to give each individual everything they will ever need with the ultimate reward being eternal life.

That ye might walk worthy of the Lord unto all pleasing, being faithful in every good work, and increasing in the knowledge of God. Strengthened with all might, according to his glorious power, unto all patience and long suffering with joyfulness.

Colossian 1:10-11

Honor

Render therefore to all their dues: tribute
to whom tribute; custom to whom custom;
fear to whom fear; honor to whom honor.

Romans 13:7

God deserves continuous praise; He is the Father of the fatherless.

Jesus blessed me with a wonderful father and mother-in-law. The Word of God enlightens us saying, *"**HONOR THY FATHER AND MOTHER; which is the first commandment with promise" (Ephesians 6:2).** Mr. David Campbell was a loving and kind man. Through my father-in-law's examples, he taught his son many important things, which were beneficial to our marriage.

Being able to observe the love in which he demonstrated to his wife, children (their spouses), grandchildren, and great grandchildren blessed me. Mr. and Mrs. Campbell were married for sixty-five years; they endured the test of time. My father-in-law was a good example to his sons, sons-in-law, grandsons, and to men in general.

Mrs. Vera Campbell was a loving and concerned person. She devoted her life to her husband, children (their spouses), grandchildren, and great grandchildren. My mother-in-law always made me feel welcomed at her home. She loved Jesus, and wanted to be pleasing to Him. Mrs. Campbell gave me many words of wisdom over the years. There were times that I told her unwise things Stan would be doing. She never expressed those concerns to him in an unconstructive way; Mrs. Campbell's actions helped us, when extremely challenging circumstances were taking place.

My mother-in-law wrote a beautiful letter to her husband, children (their spouses), grandchildren, and great grandchildren. An extremely strong statement that she declared was, "Be patient with me because God is not finished working in my life." Patience is a very important quality that every person needs to obtain. Truly think about it. Where would we be if God did not have patience with us? The Lord wants patience to have its perfect work inside of each individual's heart.

Mr. and Mrs. Campbell came to our aid; they assisted us when we were having financial difficulties. Stan and I will always be very thankful. My mother and father-in-law could perceive their children's needs and they fulfilled those necessitates if it were possible.

Thou art worthy, O Lord to receive glory and honour and power: for thou hast created all things, and for thy pleasure they are and were created.

Revelation 4:11

But ut rise, and stand upon they feet;
for I have appeared unto thee for
this propose, to make thee a minister
and a witness both of these things
which thou hast seen, and of those things
in the which I will appear unto thee:
Delivering thee from the people, and
from the Gentiles, unto whom now I
send thee, To open their eyes, and to
turn them from darkness to light,
and from the power of Satan unto
God, that they may receive forgiveness
of sins, and inheritance among them
which are sanctified by faith that is in me.

Act 26:16-18

CHAPER 11

The Vision Has Come To Pass!

*And the LORD answered me, and said, Write the
vision, and make it plain upon tables, that he may run
that readeth it. For the vision is yet for an appointed time,
but at the end it shall speak, and not lie: though it tarry,
wait for it; because it will surely come, it will not tarry.*

Habakkuk 2:2-3

Jesus is Jehovah Shalom, the God of peace. He wants each
person to have a peace that is perfect and complete with
nothing missing or broken, in every area of their lives.
**Receive the Shalom peace of God with gladness in the
name of Jesus!**

The Lord led Minister Moses Reed many times to tell me, I
should write a book; nevertheless, receiving his words was
extremely difficult to do. The things he declared sounded
impossible; God had to place that vision inside of me. I did
not have any confidence in my writing abilities, a totally
unqualified person attempting to write a book did not
make sense!

Over a period of time, I received a great desire to start this
extremely challenging responsibility. However, profound
feelings of uncertainty existed within me. Many demanding

obligations had to be done. Looking at my own inadequacy instead of the mighty power of God was extremely unwise. It took at least two years before I could truly understand and totally commit myself.

Jesus wanted to reveal Himself to people through my writings. The Word clearly states, *"Now unto him that is able to do exceeding abundantly above all that we ask or think, according to the power that worketh in us" (Ephesians 3:20).* God was going to endow me with the proficiencies that would be required; however, I needed to trust Him. *"For therein is the righteousness of God revealed from faith to faith: as it is written, the just shall live by faith" (Romans 1:17).* As a prevailing result to His influential power this vision would be successfully accomplished.

One night I gave birth to a set of triplets in a dream. In that vision Stan was so happy about the delivery of our three babies. I told a friend those things a few days later. Gwen replied, "Vickie this could be a spiritual dream." A spiritual dream sounded outstanding! With great expectation I was now looking for a triple blessing from God!

At that time I could only believe the Lord to give me a good job, new car, and nice home. However, He had assets that were far greater in mind, which began in the spiritual realm. His Word profoundly declares, *"Eye hath not seen, nor ear heard, neither have entered into the heart of man, the things which God hath prepared for them that love him. But God hath revealed them unto us by his Spirit for the Spirit searcheth all things, yea, the deep things of God" (1 Corinthians 2:9-10).* God was going to work His intoxicating power through me.

Over a period of time my dream was revealed to me, the three babies are four books. The manuscript that you are completing **WORDS FROM THE MASTER'S COLLECTION (PART 1)**, is the head of my first spiritual baby. **WORDS FROM THE MASTER'S COLLECTION (PART 2)** its body is soon to come. Chosen people of God will help me to write the next three books. Through His never ending authority they are going to do extensive damage to the powers of darkness.

The supernatural power of the Holy Ghost, faith, prayers, and God's Word helped me to become obedient to His will. Fasting, hard work, and patience were also devices that were exploited to bring this vision to pass. Over a length of time Jesus regenerated and reestablished my thoughts. It is written, *"Submit your work unto the Lord, and thy thoughts shall be established" (Proverbs 16:3).* The actions that needed to be done could only be achieved through the massive power of the Holy Ghost that He worked in me mightily.

Jesus gave me a great responsibility to write books, however, He did not want this vision to be revealed to anyone. My husband was told two months after I started to write. Stan, our children, and a dictionary helped me with my spelling. Before those things happened I would not attempt to find a word in a dictionary because of a lack of confidence in that area.

God knew there were people who would not have had a desire to rejoice with me in regards to the awesome exploits I was chosen to successfully accomplish. Satan wanted to abort and totally destroy my babies (the vision of writing books). He longed to employ any person who would surrender to his spirit. The evil one needed someone he could exploit to achieve his malicious and evil plans. **Never permit the devil to use you to hinder or stop a God given assignment!**

The Lord gave me a wonderful deed to accomplish; He deposited His thoughts inside of my mind. Jesus awesomely worked out every difficulty, which occurred. To do most of the actions that needed to be done blind faith had to be exercised. However, when I think about it now, God given faith is blind. His Word tells us, *"Now faith is the substance of things hoped for, the evidence of things not seen" (Hebrews 11:1).*

For many years I asked Jesus to prepare people's hearts to receive the writings He led me to compose. At this time my prayers are for Him to make those words burn inside of each sinner's and born again believers' hearts, which reads or hears about them. Through God's grace the unsaved will be totally delivered from their sinful way of living. The born again are going to be set free from bondages and supernaturally blessed by His mighty power. They will be a part of a countless number of people that will stand at the Judgment Set of Christ. **This is the Lord's doing and it is marvelous in my eyes!**

When people have faith and are obedient to the visions that God called them to perform; He will without a hesitation bring those things to pass. Jesus wants to empower individuals to achieve great and miraculous deeds, which appears to be absolutely impossible.

Regardless to the adversities that will take place; God has given His beloved victory in every area of their lives. *"Blessed be the God and Father of our Lord Jesus Christ who hath blessed us with all spiritual blessings in heavenly places in Christ:" "Having made known unto us the mystery of his will, according to his good pleasure which he hath purposed in himself." (Ephesians 1:3, 9)*

For I know the thoughts that I think toward you, saith the LORD, thoughts of peace and not evil, to give you an expected end.

Jeremiah 29:11

My first baby's head **WORDS FROM THE MASTER'S COLLECTION (PART 1)** has come out! I am patiently waiting for its body **WORDS FROM THE MASTER'S COLLECTION (PART 2)** to be delivered. In like manner the body of Christ is excitingly waiting for Jesus' glorious arrival. He is the Head of the church and the saints are His body. It is written, *"And hath put all things under his feet, and gave him to be the head over all things to the church. Which is his body, the fulness of him that filleth all in all"* (Ephesians 1:22-23). *"And he is the head of the body, the church: who is the beginning, the firstborn from the dead; that in all things he might have the preeminence"* (Colossians 1:18).

Jesus is in heaven sitting at the right hand of God, a day has previously been chosen for Him to return (in the sky). He is coming back to receive a church that is prepared and waiting for His miraculous and extraordinary appearance. *"And then shall appear the sign of the Son of man in heaven: and then shall all the tribes of the earth mourn, and they shall see the Son of man coming in the clouds of heaven with power and great glory. And he shall send his angels with a great sound of a trumpet, and they shall gather together his elect from the four winds, from one end of heaven to the other"* (Matthew 24:30-31).

"I come quickly; and my reward is with me, to give every man according as his work shall be. I am Al'-pha and O-me'-ga, the beginning and the end, the first and the last" *(Revelation 22:12-13).* *"Take ye heed, watch and pray: for ye know not when the time is"* *(Mark 13:33).* After the **"Day of Judgment"** God's divine kingdom and authority shall rule and reign forever. Eternal praise and glory belongs to Jesus Christ; He is the King of all kings and the Lord of all lords. Jesus is the Only Living God!

TO BE CONTINUED
TO GOD BE THE GLORY!